TO

THE ATTIC PLAYERS

*

CONTENTS

INTRODUCTION

EURIPIDES was born in 484 B.C. and died in 406. The first two thirds of his life coincided with the miraculous rise of Athenian political power and cultural creativity, the fifty years between the victories over Persia at Salamis and Plataea and the beginning of the war between Athens and Sparta in 431. The retreat of the Persian force in 479 had left the Athenians with a devastated city, but in an unquestioned position as the leaders of Greek independence; and Athens was soon the most powerful member of the Delian League, an alliance of Greek states formed to resist Persian aggression. Within a generation the treasury of the League had been transferred from Delos to Athens, and the alliance was fast becoming an Athenian empire. By 440 this empire was widely felt as a menace to the freedom it had been designed to protect – the freedom of small states and of Hellas as a whole; and Sparta, Corinth, and Thebes headed the resistance, which in 431 led to open war. Fifteen of the seventeen extant plays of Euripides were produced under the conditions imposed by this desperate struggle, which ended in 404 with total defeat. But four years before that disaster Euripides had gone into voluntary exile in Macedon, where he died early in 406.

Euripides had seen Aeschylus' *Oresteian Trilogy* when he was twenty-six. All through his productive life he competed with Sophocles in the annual festivals of Dionysus. Sophocles, eleven years older, survived him by three years; but the two men, though contemporaries, belonged to two different generations, and their works reflect two different worlds of thought and interpretation of experience. Each is aware of a supernatural reality in the midst of which man pursues his natural course; and neither credits this reality with benevolence towards mankind. But whereas in Sophocles the gods in some degree understand human thoughts and actions and on occasion take a hand in their affairs, so that reverence for them is the proper attitude of humans, Euripides presents the gods rather as symbols of amoral cosmic or social forces, blind and often destructive in their operation; powers which man can apprehend if not explain, but which are themselves incapable of understanding the spiritual qualities of man or the values by which he lives. Gods are both the beauty and the peril of life, the peremptory conditions of living, the facts of the world as it is. Men and women must accept both the benefits and the cruelties of the world, must 'endure the gift of a god'; piety is acknowledgement of fact. In Euripides' plays kindness, sympathy, and self-knowledge are more important than reverence. The reverence Aphrodite demands from us is recognition that she is a part of our nature. The cause of disaster is more often deficient humanity than want of respect for powers who do not respect the spirit of man; this is true even in *The Bacchae*. Unpredictable Chance (*Tychē*) shares with Necessity (*anankē*) the main direction of human lives, and neither of these deities can be affected by reverence or propitiation. Beyond human life, and out of reach of human thought, is Zeus, whose function is as obscure as his nature, except that he too must bow to Necessity. Sophocles treated Athena and Apollo with respect; Euripides treated Olympians – though Zeus is usually an exception – ironically. Both poets lived in their maturity through the generation of the long war; Sophocles' philosophy survived that experience; Euripides' philosophy can almost be said to have reckoned with it before it came; eight of the plays that we possess from the war period are wholly or partly concerned with the processes of war. Yet this theme only began to occupy Euripides' mind when he was well past fifty; and it did not replace, but rather enlarged and complemented, the greater theme which this poet pursued through his whole life: the relationship of man to woman.

His study of this, the most insistent and universal problem of human life, achieved a radical profundity, a freedom from conventional assumption, which was as rare in his day as it has been in every century since. To say, as some critics earlier in our own century did, that Euripides argued for the emancipation of women is untrue and beside the point; there is every indication that he accepted the ascendancy of man as an unalterable feature of society. But his plays contain, hidden below the popular surface, an appeal to men to stop deceiving themselves about the benevolence of their behaviour to women, to recognize what their assumptions and their institutions really involve. The ever-present hostility and mistrust between the sexes Euripides saw as an imprisonment warping the lives of men and women equally.

His criticism of man's behaviour to woman is somewhat more severe than his criticism of woman's behaviour to man simply because man's accepted position gives him power and initiative. The fact that Euripides was known in his day as a hater of women and not as a hater of men simply reflects the fact that the majority of men in his audience, watching the behaviour of Jason, Hippolytus, Admetus, Demophon, Agamemnon, Orestes, did not feel that these heroes' acts and attitudes were greatly unlike their own or were being held up for censure at all; while in watching Phaedra many of them knew at once that she was a whore, and did not trouble to listen to her words, which show her as a passionately moral woman. And it is not unfair to say that many scholars who in the past century and a half have interpreted these plays for the less learned have done so from a social standpoint comparable with that of the average Athenian of Euripides' day; while in fact one purpose to which Euripides' work as a whole is dedicated is to hold up to ironic question and criticism the attitude to life and its problems held by most men in his audience. Many received opinions about these plays owe their acceptance today to the inertia which has prevailed ever since they were first formulated by men of excellent formal scholarship in a period when Greek was studied and taught almost exclusively in male universities with a Christian foundation, and when a reader such as the poet Shelley was vilified, persecuted, and exiled.

Between 455 and 428 B.C. Euripides wrote, as far as we know, nearly thirty plays, of which three have survived complete: *Alcestis* (438), *Medea* (431), and *Hippolytus* (428). From fragments and other information we know that about twenty of these earlier plays took as their main theme the sufferings or the misdeeds of women in heroic legend. From 428 onward an increasingly prominent place in Euripides' plots was taken by the whole subject of war; but in this period more than half of the surviving plays, and at least five of those known to us from fragments, dealt also specifically with woman's relation to man and man's behaviour to woman. The three plays in this volume provide enough evidence for a critical reader to begin to understand the way the poet worked, offering to his audience portraits and situations which it was easy to interpret in a traditional sense, but which if examined more closely led to a questioning of some basic assumptions of social life.

This kind of study of Euripides' plays will in general not be found in the standard books on Greek drama, which tend to be more concerned with questions of development in style and structure, and to deny that we can reach any useful conclusion about the poet's message or meaning in questions of social or personal morality. An attitude of this kind, when the author under discussion is one who deals passionately with the most fundamental moral questions, is unsatisfactory and detracts seriously from the interest and value of studying this author. His plays convey a detailed comment on the relationship of men and women, with clear moral implications. They voice an outspoken criticism of the purposes and processes of war. They examine the operation of conscious guilt, and of the thirst for revenge, in individuals and in society; and explore the possibilities of a notion for which the word came into use only during the poet's lifetime: *syngnōmē*, pardon. A further area of morality is investigated in those plays which deal with five legendary examples of human sacrifice; another in the eight plays which include men and women who express their feelings about Helen of Sparta. The whole question of the meaning of freedom is analysed in a number of plays; sometimes in the behaviour of slaves, sometimes in the things that free men say about their own freedom, and the way their actions betray their loss of it. All of these themes. except that of war, are exemplified in the three plays translated here: if in any one case the author's meaning and message are not fully clarified, that is because we have here only one sixth of his extant work. Study of the rest will reveal a consistent and coherent outlook on the world and on human life giving to each play purpose, dramatic power, and relevance to the current experience of the author's fellow-Athenians.

The chief reason why some of Euripides' plays have so often been described as self-contradictory, obscure, or careless, is also one reason why scholars have been reluctant to find a consistent moral outlook in his writing. It is his use of irony. To say that Euripides uses irony is a commonplace; but the kind of irony commonly recognized in his plays is only a small part of it. In *Iphigenia in Tauris*, just after we have seen Orestes enter with Pylades, Iphigenia recounts her dream and mourns for her brother's death; when Orestes stands a prisoner expecting death, he wishes that the hand of his sister (he means Electra) might prepare his body for burial. This kind of thing was a theatrical technique, and of no great significance. The more characteristic Euripidean irony is seen, for example, in the fact that Iphigenia bitterly blames her father for sacrificing her, but, though shocked by Orestes' matricide, she neither censures him for it nor sees it as a logical cause of Orestes' sufferings, though he himself has stated (573-5) that he must have been mad when he did it. It is seen again in the irrationality of Iphigenia's conclusion that, because she has been told that Orestes was alive many months ago when the strangers left Argos, her last night's dream of his death must be a false message. Other and more significant examples will be observed as we study *Hippolytus* and *Alcestis*; but some of the most powerfully ironic plays are contained in the volume entitled *Orestes and Other Plays*,[1] where the ironic method can be examined in detail.

Above all, Euripides uses irony in his depiction of the way men think and speak about women; and with this goes also the way most women speak about women, since women adopt men's assumptions in this matter as the only basis for an acceptable life in a community organized almost entirely by men. Thus *Hippolytus* ends with the sanctified apotheosis of a man whose virtue has expressed itself not in noble severity but in fanatical cruelty, whose central principle of life is a destructive evasion of life's central responsibility; a man who is, by his own account, obsessed with hatred of women. The tender sympathy shown for him by Artemis, by Theseus, by the chorus of Trozenian women, endorses the self-regard and self-pity which have already appeared in some of Hippolytus' lines. The prince forgives his father for causing his death; but who is he to bestow pardon, instead of asking it for the death which his own inordinate hatred has led to? Phaedra had not full self-knowledge, but she struggled hard for it and achieved it in an honourable degree; Hippolytus has none. The only serious moral searching in the play occurs in the debate between Phaedra and the Nurse. Each of these women has a share of both truth and error; and the passion of Phaedra's fight for integrity and goodness is measured by the wickedness she resorts to when chance and cruelty defeat her. All this is entirely forgotten in the male world of the final scenes, where our attention is engrossed by two heroes both incapable of understanding the anguish we witnessed in the woman's world with which the play began. This is the scale, and the

1. Penguin Books, 1972.

level, on which Euripides' irony operates. The truths he had to suggest
were so far beyond the imagination of any but a handful of his listeners
and readers that irony of this kind was the only possible way of expressing his beliefs. A great poet writes first for himself, next for those
who will search for his deepest meaning, and last for the rest. It is
true that the critic who interprets a play as irony may be charged
with making his own rules as he goes along; it is equally true that
irony by definition can appeal only to the imagination. To deny that
the irony is there, to insist that the naïve, direct interpretation is the
whole meaning of the text, is to find oneself facing the familiar set of
obscurities, levities, and contradictions in Euripides' work which have
led so many critics to censure, apologize for, and patronize this
dramatist.

If, then, the poet's inner message was addressed to so few, why was
he so popular with the many that far more of his work survived than
of either Aeschylus or Sophocles? Chiefly for one good reason and for
one less good. The good reason is the power of his poetry – the limpid
directness of his dialogue, but still more the beauty of his lyric
choruses. Ordinary people read them and learnt them by heart;
Athenian soldiers enslaved at Syracuse earned freedom by reciting
them. The three plays in this book include some of the loveliest
examples. The less good reason is the novelty, variety, and pathos of
his plots and situations. These are, of course, legitimate qualities; the
romantic recognition, the intrigue for escape, will hold an audience
in any age. But this is a less good reason because in many cases such
elements are an ironic cover for deeper meanings of which the average
spectator or reader was unaware. The listener to *Hippolytus* who was
prepared (like Aeschylus in Aristophanes' *Frogs*) to label Phaedra a
whore would be unable to comprehend the ironic meaning of the
epilogue; still more in such plays as *The Children of Heracles* or *Orestes*
the poet's real message, if not veiled by irony, might have caused
perilous offence. Certainly most modern interpretation has failed to
come to terms with this vital character of Euripides' work. Yet we
must remember that the dramatist wrote for his popular audience,
whose national festival it was, as well as for those few who looked
eagerly for unpalatable truth. One reason why his plays are of living
interest today is that some of his central truths are still unpalatable.

Other qualities in addition to formal scholarship are necessary for those who mean to discover his method and explore his meaning.

ALCESTIS (438 B.C.)

Because much of *Alcestis* is written in unusually simple Greek it has often been the first play read by beginners in the language; as a result, perhaps also because of the fairy-tale quality of the story, it has sometimes been regarded as an elementary piece of work – a judgement which is now being abandoned. The astonishing completeness, symmetry, and subtlety of its structure have been demonstrated in two expositions, almost opposite in sense, and both valuable, which any student wishing to explore this play and to begin an understanding of Euripides would be well advised to read. The first is W. D. Smith's 'The Ironic Structure in *Alcestis*',[1] and the other is A. P. Burnett's 'The Virtues of Admetus'.[2] A study of two such careful yet contradictory views will not only stimulate the reader's enjoyment of this play; it will also demonstrate how probable it is that this and other plays of the same author could, when they first appeared, convey widely different meanings both to those who read and discussed them, and still more to those who attended the single first performance in the Dionysiac Theatre – and these were certainly the majority. When a spectator's attention is claimed simultaneously by décor, music, choreography, acting style, poetry, suspense, his time for interpreting meaning is limited; and Euripides was clearly aware of this. In reading him we should always be prepared to find one meaning accessible to those capable of reflection, and another offered to those who sought only entertainment. The Athenian dramatist provided in the first place a religious observance; and in this he combined spectacle for the eye, release for the emotions, and food for thought. In a gathering of many thousands each had the right to decide what the play meant for him at that moment; the student must attempt the longer task of seeing gradually more and more of the author's meaning.

1. Reprinted from *Phoenix* XIV (1960) in *Euripides' Alcestis*, edited by J. R. Wilson, Prentice-Hall, 1968.
2. Reprinted from *Classical Philology* LX, no. 4, October 1965, in *Euripides*, edited by Erich Segal, Prentice-Hall, 1968.

The theme of *Alcestis* is the inexorable power of Necessity (*anankē*); and the story presents this theme in two aspects: the absolute impact of death, and the insoluble dilemma of marriage. The marriage here presented is not, as in *Medea*, a 'problem' marriage, but a particularly successful one, in which husband and wife, each as loving and as virtuous as the other, after establishing a model home and a promising family, are confronted with Necessity in the form of a sickness which threatens the life of Admetus. The legend said that Apollo, in return for Admetus' kindness during his year of servitude, persuaded the Fates to allow him to 'escape imminent death if he could find another to take his place'. Admetus accepted this chance of escape, and asked his old parents, and other relatives, to die for him. When they refused, hs wife Alcestis offered herself. The original story said that the sickness, Apollo's bargain, and Alcestis' offer, all occurred on Admetus' wedding-day. Euripides made a significant change: the payment of the debt of a life in exchange for Admetus' life was postponed for an unspecified period; so that the action takes place on the day of Alcestis' death, which has been long expected; and the story of Apollo's bargain has become widely known (523–4). By establishing this interval the dramatist presents us with a marriage which has continued for some time under this accepted condition, and which can thus serve as a subject for study.

Study may begin at a point which the poet deliberately left unmentioned (as Burnett rightly insists): the crucial moment when Admetus accepted his wife's offer to die in his place. He may have asked her, as he asked his parents, or she may have offered unasked; the latter seems a natural inference from the text, as is the supposition that Admetus, once he had agreed in principle to Apollo's proposal, was bound to accept whatever life was offered. The only hint given is the statement of the chorus at 1071 that 'you must endure the gift of a god'. The point is not clarified, because for us to form a clear moral judgement on Admetus would limit the significance of the play to a particular and improbable case. The theme of the play is bigger than the story of Admetus; it is the whole unequal relationship of man to woman, shown in its most common and characteristic institution, marriage – and in marriage at its best.

In the first scene the serving-maid reports Alcestis' words spoken with tears to her marriage-bed: 'I am dying because I cannot bear to fail in my duty to you and to my husband.' This view of a wife's duty the chorus recognize as being an ideal which is generally accepted and thought honourable; which in principle every husband would regard as his due, without ever expecting to see it fulfilled. The ideal of marriage, in fact, carries to its conclusion the universal assumption that a woman's life is a rational price for a man's life, being of less value; that the women of a family are expendable, their lives at the disposal of the men's lives (see e.g. *Iph. Taur.* 1005–6). Admetus has never questioned this principle and is therefore hardly aware of it. Alcestis did not set this ideal for herself, but finding it already part of the fabric of society she embraced it with a thoroughness which was her own rare and heroic achievement.

We see, then, that even if it was theoretically possible for Admetus to decline, yet when his wife made the offer it would actually seem to him to be above all things *right* – right in a degree beyond the achievement of most men's wives. To refuse it would seem to flout an order of nature and to annul a gesture of unique beauty. The chorus of Pheraean Elders take the same view, and there is little doubt that almost the whole of the original audience shared this view and ignored the only two people in the play who question it – the two slaves. It was so obvious that this self-sacrifice showed the perfection of wifehood, the consummation of an ideal marriage. In presenting this situation Euripides does not say it is wrong, nor that it is right; rather he asks, What are the effects of this institution whose ideal pattern we all accept? He shows us marriage suddenly faced with the *anankē*, the peremptory fact, of death; and the woman loses her life, but gains immortal glory, while the man keeps his life and loses everything that makes it worth keeping. To the man who asks, Where did Admetus go wrong? the answer is that society's accepted valuation of woman gives man a false sense of merited privilege, and plants contradiction in the very concept of marriage. The play shows the social principle of male ascendancy, established partly by nature and partly by man's power to organize the world for his own purposes, resulting in man's shame and confusion.

The life of a free woman in fifth-century Athens could well be an enviable one, especially if her husband's family possessed the stability given by wealth. This side of a woman's life is reflected in the earlier part of the Servant's description of how Alcestis spent the hours before

her death. These lines show Alcestis as the mother of a family, the
mistress of a large household, the possessor of an elegant and com-
fortable life, a queen who is also priestess at her own altars, and who
inaugurates this significant day alone, without her husband. This part
of the narrative ends with

> No tear fell, not a sigh was heard.

Then, says the Servant, she went into her room, and knelt by her
marriage-bed, and wept passionately for a long time, 'till the whole
coverlet was wet'.

> 'O marriage-bed,' she cried,
> 'Farewell! Here once I gave my maidenhood to him;
> And now my life. I do not hate you; yet you have
> Killed me, since I alone would not be false to you
> And to my husband; and for this I die.'

Here is the other side. The bed symbolizes the essential relationship
of man and woman; and at the heart of that relationship is an acknow-
ledged inequality. Admetus' bed is the one that Alcestis' father chose
for her; probably he could not have chosen better; but in marriage
Alcestis entered the central institution of a male society; and because
her nature is heroic her destiny lies not in its fortunate surface but
in its underlying essence. If *Alcestis* were the only play of Euripides
that had survived, it would be extravagant to suggest such an interpretation; but a study of his whole work, from the early fragments to
Iphigenia in Aulis, reveals this theme as his constant preoccupation.

It is often remarked that this play is more concerned with Admetus
than with his wife. This is true; Alcestis is simply a queen who accepts
heroically the final implication of marriage. The choice she has to
make is hard but simple, and is already made when the play opens.
Admetus too has made a choice; and because he made it too easily, the
action confronts him with a succession of further choices, each more
complex than the last. His motives in choosing also vary, but one
element is constant: the sense of guilt which becomes more articulate
and more comprehensive as the play proceeds. The painfulness of this
theme is softened by the supernatural opening and the miraculous
close of the play; these provide for the tragic tableau a frame which, at
the cost of a gentle shift between realism and make-believe, trans-

forms it. Into a hopeless and real situation the wished-for and unreal intervention of divine power brings hope. The truth of marital affection justifies this hope and promises 'a new and better life' (1157); and this scene sensitively acted on today's stage is always a moving experience. But the happy ending belongs to the touching beauty of the play, and not to life outside the theatre. In 438 B.C. Heracles' fight with Death was as much a fairy-tale as King Arthur is to us. The last phrases of reality which the audience had to remember were Admetus' question, 'Friends, what have I to live for?' and the chorus's answer, 'There is no remedy against Necessity' (960, 965).

This question and the answer come just before the final scene in which Heracles provides a triumphant 'remedy against Necessity'. The real and the unreal are equally the dramatist's tools, and in a work of art fantasy can point obliquely to truth. As Heracles departs after telling us his story of the wrestling beside the tomb, we recall that when he first arrived he made fun of the Elders for believing silly fairy-tales. In this flickering light the guilt of Admetus can be revealed without harshness; the irony is gentle, not bitter. And the guilt is not only the king's; irony is directed also at the Elders, since they represent the society of whose accepted standards Admetus is an honourable example. The Servant's narrative in the first episode displays Euripides' power to evoke pity for suffering mortals; then the Servant goes in, and the Elders begin their chant. It is as though they had heard nothing, had been blind to the picture which has moved some of the audience to tears. That picture is not these men's picture of the situation; they have their own, which remains unaffected by what a slave says. They now pray to Apollo to show mercy – to Admetus; they say to Admetus, 'How you suffer, bereft of your wife!' What calls for tears is not that Alcestis dies, but that 'the king shall see her die' (232-3). In the line that follows they speak with sorrow of the woman; but return at once (240-43) to the sufferings of the man. What is the point of this contrast? It sets the man's view against the woman's view. If modern critics notice this contrast at all, they tend to find the Elders mildly one-sided in their attitude, rather than painfully comic; and it seems even less likely that the original audience laughed at expressions which voiced what was substantially their own judgement. A man is lucky if he possesses a wife like Alcestis, and her death is for the moment a serious loss – but, whatever may be said now, in time the loss will prove reparable, as Heracles says in the last scene. When a different angle on the same general view is expressed in coarse terms by Pheres – 'With a woman like that, marriage pays; otherwise it's a bad bargain' – the words are clearly ignoble. But in that scene line after line shows (as Browning pointed out in *Balaustion's Adventure*) the painful similarities between son and father; it is the image in the mirror that kindles Admetus' rage. Then his rage is transformed by anguish into self-knowledge, because he is a man capable of learning, and capable of the sense of guilt for learning too late. Even Admetus' self-knowledge is forced upon him by hard facts rather than by moral perception; but only those few in the audience who were at least as honest as Admetus can have known how deep a question was being opened before them.

In *Alcestis* we are given a picture which we shall find yet more clearly drawn in *Hippolytus*, of two worlds living side by side: the world of free males, and the world of women and slaves – for between 'free' women and slaves there is an instinctive alliance, recognizable in play after play of Euripides. Each world lives by the mutual support of its members – Admetus, Heracles, and the Elders in the one case, Alcestis and the two slaves in the other. Here, as again in *Hippolytus*, what is remarkable is the lack of communication between the one world and the other. Heracles' feat is performed for Admetus; Alcestis gives her life ostensibly for Admetus, but – as her speech makes clear to the audience – still more for her children, who are the real centre of her world. The only true communication comes in the last scene, when speech is forbidden, and Admetus knows his wife by the touch of her hand. Doubtless many Athenian men in Euripides' day achieved understanding with their wives and learnt to honour women; and the beautiful relief-sculptures of women on many funeral tablets are often, and rightly, adduced as evidence of this. But the social scales were heavily weighted against such achievement. The sculptor or the vase-painter naturally chose for his subjects the creative and generous aspects of the life he saw around him; the only artist whose business it was to record the reverse of the coin was the dramatist; therefore his evidence is crucial, and not to be held of less value than the sculptor's. The truth Euripides expressed in his plays about the life of women was one which his world could not conceive; for it concerned the profound failure of man to form a society in which he could live on peaceful and constructive terms with the other half of the human race. And similar failure on the part of so many societies in our own day explains very simply why the theme to which Euripides dedicated so large a proportion of his life's work has even now not been generally recognized.

Comment on this play usually includes some discussion of its *genre*. It was fairly common practice for a poet to present a set of four plays, the first three being of a serious nature and more or less closely related in their subject-matter, while the fourth was a 'satyr-play'. An example of this kind of play survives in Euripides' *Cyclops*, where the chorus consists of satyrs and the plot is a humorous version of Odysseus' famous adventure in Polyphemus' cave. *Alcestis* was the fourth play in a set, of which the first three survive only in fragments. Since drunken jollity in one form or another was a regular feature of a satyr-play, Heracles' second scene seems intended to indicate, to those who wished to look no further, that this – in spite of its serious first episode – is their satyr-play, and they may enjoy it as such. The popular image of Heracles as a comedy strong man with a huge appetite (this is the figure we meet in Aristophanes' *Frogs*) made it natural that each of Heracles' scenes in *Alcestis* should include its share of comedy. But the greater part of this play is in the full tragic vein. The immortals of the prologue, and the outrageous quarrel between father and son in the third episode, may cause a wry smile; but the theme is a dying woman, a despairing man, and the relentless law of Necessity. If the interpretation of *Alcestis* suggested here is a sound one, the poet chose the half-semblance of a satyr-play in order to make it easy for any who would be offended by the true meaning to miss it altogether. It was a message which in many societies of our own day is as pertinent as it was then; and this fact itself suggests that the message was received by very few; that in human society, ancient or modern, serious radical comment on the institution of marriage, though acceptable among the select readers of philosophical works (such as Plato's *Republic*), is unwelcome to the majority of citizens, and therefore in a popular medium like the theatre needs a decent cloak of irony.

Euripides' ability to convey serious meaning through comedy is not confined to *Alcestis*; it may be seen in *Andromache*, *Ion*, *The Bacchae*, *Iphigenia in Aulis*. This poet understood, as Shakespeare did, the nervous link that joins laughing with crying. In *Alcestis* a further theatrical use is made of Heracles' drunkenness. When the Slave at last reveals the truth that Alcestis is dead, a magnificent opportunity occurs for a powerful actor to convince an audience that nothing is impossible; to transform himself in a single speech of twenty-four lines ('Come now, my endlessly enduring heart and hand . . .') from a tipsy mortal to a demi-god. This unexpected and triumphant reversal of tone makes it possible for a sensitive listener, in the scene which follows, to witness the despair of Admetus with confidence that hope will return. Realism and fantasy, irony and tenderness, complement each other. This play cannot be classified; its design is faultless and unique.

HIPPOLYTUS (428 B.C.)

The moral of *Hippolytus*, it is often said, is that you cannot fly in the face of Nature; that the person who tries to live without recognizing Aphrodite will come to a bad end, just as Pentheus in *The Bacchae* comes to a bad end because he rejects Dionysus. But such an account of the play is inadequate, and only partly true. To begin with, it is not easy to fit Artemis into this pattern. In the second place, though Hippolytus' death may have been contrived at long range by Aphrodite, as she claims in the prologue, the subsequent action shows it as due to a series of four human errors: the Nurse's foolishness, Hippolytus' fanatical cruelty, Phaedra's indignant revenge, and Theseus' impatient yielding to an irritation and jealousy which have evidently been long restrained. Our interest in these errors obliterates any sense that matters are being divinely organized. The two goddesses, representing elemental forces in human nature, provide a pleasing and powerful structure to the drama. But the drama itself is not primarily about the indulgence or the repression of the sexual urge, or even about human errors such as those just mentioned. Its first theme is *syngnōmē*, pardon; and its second is the deep gulf of misunderstanding which divides men from women. The first theme is summarized in the Nurse's appeal to Hippolytus (615):

Forgive, son; we are human, we do wrong by nature.

The second is summarized in Phaedra's words (669):

How cruel a curse it is to be born a woman!

The Greek word for 'pardon' (both verb and noun) appears for the first time in writers of the mid-fifth century, chiefly Sophocles and Euripides; and in a number of Euripides' plays, which show the disasters that follow from the blind pursuit of revenge, *syngnōmē* became an important *motif*. It is treated more fully in *Hippolytus* than in any other extant play. In *Alcestis*, though the word itself is not used, the idea is clearly present in the resolution of Admetus' guilt towards both Heracles and Alcestis. The idea, and the word, have a significant place in *The Women of Troy* (950, 1043) and in *Electra* (1105). In the last scene of *The Bacchae* ruined mortals beg for pardon from an insulted god, and are rejected. But in *Hippolytus* every mortal character is concerned with pardon – with bestowing, receiving, withholding, or urging it.

Before we look at scenes in detail, we should distinguish carefully between the Christian notion of 'forgiveness' (not *syngnōmē* but *aphesis*, 'remission') and 'pardon' as Euripides understood it. 'Forgiveness' involves a positive emotional attitude of forgiver to forgiven – often a mutual relationship because it acts in response to repentance. *Syngnōmē*, on the contrary, is less emotional – is simply the decision to cease anger and renounce reprisal; a civilized attitude towards past fact. A second distinction is that Christian forgiveness is bestowed by one who feels himself indebted to God for the pardon of his own sins; thus the emotion is twofold, of receiving and of bestowing. The Christian notion is complex and essentially religious. For Olympian gods such a relationship to mortals is impossible, though mortals are reluctant to recognize this. Therefore the notion of pardon in Euripides is simple and without religious implications, operating between one mortal and another.

Aphrodite in the prologue states that she intends to punish Hippolytus' neglect of her with death. When Hippolytus enters and expresses his total disregard for Aphrodite, the old slave gently remonstrates with him and then, left alone, prays to Aphrodite to forgive the young man's rash words. Mortals, he knows, are seldom wise enough to forgive, but 'gods ought to be wiser than mortals'. Thus the prologue establishes the issue between reprisal and pardon as the matter of the play. The mortal thinks that because he himself understands the wisdom of pardon a god must understand it too; but Aphrodite has already shown us that it is outside her comprehension. A

century after Euripides Aristotle, identifying the intellectual part of
man's nature with the divine, exhorted men 'to become, as far as
possible, like the immortals' (*Ethics* 10.7); but this view, which began
with Plato, is the opposite of that general view of the world which
was implicit in Homer and received its clearest expression in Euripides.
For Euripides, gods represent the unalterable forces of human nature,
society, and the physical cosmos – the sublime, unfeeling, amoral
facts of existence, among which man must survive as best he can;
while wisdom, goodness, love, courage, every aspiration towards the
ideal – these have their sole source in the hearts of human beings,
whether slaves or princes. Man desires to believe that his own goodness reflects the goodness of the world, that gods can be generous or
trustworthy; but he is wrong. (The chorus in *Hippolytus* do not make
this mistake; they fear (145–50) that Phaedra's sickness may be due
to some resentment on the part of Artemis.) This play shows a self-
repeating cycle of anger, reprisal, suffering, and more anger; the one
sadly limited, but genuine, act of pardon shown is achieved in the last
scene by two mortals after divinity has departed.

When Phaedra first begins to tell the Nurse her secret (337–43) she
speaks of her mother Pasiphaë and her sister Ariadne; memory and
heredity exact their debts, which Phaedra knows she will have to pay.
This is the very point where she is closest to Hippolytus; both are
young idealists, and each remembers a mother who had felt the cruelty
of Aphrodite. When Hippolytus in 1082 says,

> My unhappy mother! In what bitterness I was born!

it seems clear that he is revealing the unconscious and irrational cause
of that hatred of women which flamed from him in his second scene
and led first to Phaedra's death and then to his. Theseus, when he
discovers Phaedra dead, at first remembers, as she did, the unforgiving
power of past fact (831–3)

> From some distant age,
> From sin committed in time long past,
> I reap this harvest which the gods have sent.

Phaedra will not forgive the Nurse; the pathos lies in the fact that this
matters so little, because she is a slave. We do not expect Phaedra to
forgive Hippolytus. Hippolytus will forgive neither woman. Nor can

Theseus hesitate a moment to punish his son. When Artemis tells Theseus (1326) that he may be pardoned because of his ignorance, she means merely that no further disaster is to fall on him; her own blindness to the idea of pardon is shown by 1331–4 and 1420–21. Her instruction to Hippolytus 'not to hate his father' comes when Hippolytus has already shown (1405–9) that it is unnecessary.

The pardon which Hippolytus gives to his father is honourable, and is balanced by Theseus' penitence; but it does not suggest that Hippolytus has learnt any lesson from the day's disasters. He ignores Artemis' reference to Phaedra (1404–5). He accepts as a secondary cause of his death his father's anger (1413), laying prime responsibility on Aphrodite (1401, 1415). It does not occur to him that either his intense hatred of women in general, or his cruelty to Phaedra in particular, might be partly to blame (nor does this occur to the chorus). He forgives Theseus as a fellow-victim, not as a fellow-sinner. He dies fully convinced of the perfection of his own character, and no one contradicts him.

The second theme in Hippolytus is the gulf of non-communication which divides the male and the female worlds. We observed in *Alcestis* that slaves may have perceptions which unite them with women rather than with men. At the end of the prologue of *Hippolytus* the old slave separates himself from the group of young hunters, and his words introduce the women's world which then enters. The chorus talk of the queen's sickness, and of women's troubles. From then on, for fully half of the play, the stage is occupied by women, with the single intrusion of woman's enemy in the person of Hippolytus. This half of the play contains two superb choral odes: the famous poem to love, and the despairing cry for escape from a world where love leads to suicide. It contains Phaedra's painful and scrupulous search for self-knowledge, and her statement of the pure and noble life as she understands it; as well as the Nurse's robust recognition of physiological fact and practical compromise. The courage and honesty of this world are admirable, its error is excusable, its wickedness grossly provoked. When Phaedra is dead, we are in a male world until the end of the play. By comparison it is a shallow world. Again excusable error leads to disaster – but here the excuse is given divine recognition. For Phaedra's self-knowledge we have Hippolytus' self-righteousness which deceives not only himself but the chorus of women who forget how he hated and despised them. No truth about the nature of gods or the springs of human action is explored. Error is dispelled by divine revelation, but the hatred which was a deeper cause of disaster is never arraigned. Theseus and his son are reconciled, too late; and both have forgotten the earlier death which the one had briefly mourned, and the other caused. In this male world there is less truth, less response to truth, less universal interest, than in the world of women. This two-sided picture is found also both earlier and later, in two such different plays as *Medea* and *Helen*. It is, for Euripides, the one fact of human life which above all others needs to be presented repeatedly and in all its aspects to the consideration of citizens. In the world of women the notion of pardon finds little place – the Nurse pleads for it, and is repulsed; in the male world it finds real though limited scope; between the two worlds, where it is most needed, it cannot operate at all. Phaedra says that to be a woman is to be *misēma pasin*, an object of general hatred (Creusa says much the same thing in *Ion*); Hippolytus confirms that for him at least this is true; and the play ends with his apotheosis. In comparison with such a theme – the human race divided into two enemy camps, made for love but dedicated to hate – the war of the two goddesses, the issue of indulgence or abstinence, becomes superficial. Here too the dramatist's irony allows each listener or reader to perceive as much as he is ready to perceive, and to leave what he cannot use.

Or the matter can be put a different way. Theseus speaks cruel words rashly, not understanding the true situation. They result in the death of a young man. When Artemis reveals the true situation, Theseus is shattered by self-reproach; he repents, and receives pardon from his son. Hippolytus speaks cruel words rashly, not understanding the true situation. They result in the death of a young woman. When Artemis reveals the true situation, Hippolytus utters not one word of self-reproach; he remains unconscious of the cruelty of his speech; nor does Theseus, or the chorus, reproach him. Instead they load him with praises, and the agony of Phaedra is forgotten. Phaedra is not even censured for her false accusation; she is ignored, and the play ends in an exclusively male world from which the reality of death – which ought to have united Hippolytus and Phaedra in tragic sympathy – excludes even the bloodless Artemis. The rarity of comment on this ironic pattern suggests that our world today does not entirely reject the assumptions of the ancient world about the relative importance of a man's life and a woman's life; and explains why the similar irony which pervades Euripides' work is so little understood.

One reason for the popularity of this play among both readers and performers is the character of the Nurse. She is an anonymous slave, yet she has a longer part than anyone except Hippolytus. She is foolish, yet her foolishness is no more remarkable than the rashness of Theseus. She advocates deception and indulgence; but not for her own profit. There is no cruelty in her, and she knows that mortals must forgive. She fatally misunderstands both Phaedra and Hippolytus; but she understands Aphrodite as no one else does. So, with the freedom that belongs (as Euripides frequently demonstrates) only to slaves, she alone is able to pose a profound issue underlying this drama: which kind of value is the more absolute, or the more relative – that based on a cosmic apprehension of Aphrodite, or that based on loyalty to a social or personal ideal? The system of values for which Phaedra dies is one which involves the subservience of woman. Part of the function of the two goddesses in the dramatic design is that each in her own way denies that subservience. When the Nurse creeps away with Phaedra's malediction in her ears, she wins as little approval from the audience as, in the end, the two goddesses. Yet in her very want of refinement grows an admirable vitality; and for all her misjudgement and her dishonesty, the fact remains that the audience could learn from her more needed truth, and more humanity, than from anyone else on the stage.[1]

IPHIGENIA IN TAURIS (413 or 412 B.C.)

The standard accounts of this play describe its particular interest under two headings: the religious and the romantic. The religious interest is illustrated by reference to such lines as 1015–16, where Orestes says, 'Now I begin to see Apollo's purpose'; and the 'happy ending' is

1. For a different view of the Nurse see W. S. Barrett's edition of *Hippolytus*, (Oxford, Clarendon Press, 1964), page 194: 'This old miscreant . . . deeply attached to Phaedra, but impatient, domineering, and with no moral scruple.' This combines the judgements made by Phaedra and by Hippolytus; but it is unlikely that the author intended the portrait to be so one-sided. On the play in general, and on most details, Barrett's commentary is among the best available on any Greek play, and essential to the student.

taken as expressing the poet's conviction that divine power overrules human error to establish peace and justice. The romantic interest is said to stir tender emotions by the reunion of severed affection, by the intriguing escape from danger, and by the fantasy of a strange and remote country. This general view, however, may well be superficial, and represent an aspect of the play intended for the less reflective members of the original audience rather than for those with whom the poet was most concerned to communicate. The religious attitude described is, I believe, ironic, and the author's meaning therefore the opposite to that usually ascribed to him; while the romantic elements, though certainly there and available for those ready to respond to them, are of small interest by comparison with the important themes whose interweaving forms the main structure of this play.

There are four main themes. The first is the story underlying the plot – the story of the accursed House of Atreus, and of one fatal event in that story – the sacrifice of Iphigenia by Agamemnon. The second theme is the reaction of one woman to the pattern of events dictated by that curse, and this is shown in a detailed depiction of Iphigenia's character which demands our study. The third theme is a topical one which, after nearly twenty years of war, was being poignantly felt all over Hellas – the misery of exile and the sorrows of severed families; and the fourth is an objective comment on the accepted view of the difference between Greeks and barbarians.

It is simplest to begin with the second theme, the character of Iphigenia. This is developed with the kind of fullness and precision exemplified already in at least half-a-dozen female characters from *Alcestis* to *Electra*. Iphigenia is pictured for us in three relationships – to Artemis, to Agamemnon, and to other people in general. Each of these shows a complexity which is contrasted with the one simple and pure element in her composition – the love and devotion she feels towards Orestes. (A similar pattern, though in harsher colours, appears in the portrait of Electra in *Orestes*, produced four years later than this play.)

In the prologue Iphigenia tells her own story. 'My father sacrificed me, for Helen's sake, to Artemis.' She is describing events of nearly twenty years ago. Her father had been ready to obey a divine command to kill her; and she, after being promised the most enviable of marriages, and then subjected to the ordeal of ritual slaughter, had been saved by the goddess from physical death and condemned for twenty years to enforced virginity and spiritual death in a remote land where a barbarous king imposed barbarous rituals of death in the name of the goddess. In the prologue Iphigenia has no doubt that the Taurians' human sacrifices are performed by divine will: they are (line 35) 'rites which Artemis takes pleasure in'. Earlier she had ascribed the bloodthirsty command at Aulis only to the priest Calchas (16ff.); but Calchas had no part in appointing her to preside over human sacrifice in Taurica, and in 224ff. she does not acquit Artemis. So, in 258-9 her words,

> The altar of Artemis is not yet dyed too deep
> with streams of Hellene blood,

indicate a satisfaction that cruelty is paid with cruelty, and give to the savage will of Artemis the same endorsement which we find again in 348-58.

But the long speech (342-91) in which this last passage occurs is in itself a complex dramatic and psychological development of central significance in the play. When she begins, Iphigenia is full of bitterness – against Fate for Orestes' death, against Hellas, against Artemis. She thinks with satisfaction of the death the two Greek strangers will suffer, and only wishes that her victims could include Helen or Menelaus. Her anger then concentrates on her last memory of her father at Aulis. From this she passes to thoughts of the home she left to go to Aulis; and the tenderness of that memory transforms her whole mood. She forgets her thirst for revenge, acquits Artemis, recognizes that murder is evil; and concludes that human sacrifice merely reflects the barbarity of those who practise it. After the choral ode, as the strangers are led in, the chorus echo her thought – that such barbarity distinguishes Taurians from Greeks. It is left to the audience to remember that the sacrifice undertaken by Agamemnon was worse than those which Thoas practises, in that it involved kin-murder.

Yet Iphigenia, in her deprived and lonely position, understandably depends on Artemis, and finds in her priesthood the confidence which she should have found in her city if she had one. Memories of home give her confidence to assert that the Artemis she serves is not, either in Hellas or in Taurica, a bloodthirsty god; the confidence to choose, if not to create, the deity she will worship. Her prayer in 1230-33 is at last true piety, because its spiritual basis is not any received tradition but a human judgement reached through the experience of suffering.

Euripides can portray true piety; but being himself a realist he cannot ascribe to it a value it does not possess. When all prayers for help to Apollo and Artemis come to their final test, when Iphigenia stands on the deck of Orestes' ship and states that if Artemis is, as her priestess believes, 'not evil', she must uphold human standards:

> You, goddess, love your own
> Brother; believe that I too love my nearest kin!

– then at last it is made clear that piety is a false guide. Both Agamemnon and Orestes had denied their own judgement in the name of piety. If gods can guide us in moral perplexity they can save us in physical peril; if they cannot save us in physical peril they cannot guide us in moral perplexity. Apollo, the Messenger reports, was as heedless, or powerless, as Artemis; and the ship drove helplessly to the shore and to the comprehensive fate promised by Thoas. Thus the play is moving, as surely as Orestes' ship, to an end whose depressing horror is undeniably appropriate to the story unfolded in the play's earlier scenes and illustrated by Orestes' insane fit, which the Herdsman witnessed on the shore. The goddess Athena, who here, as in *The Suppliant Woman* and *Ion*, speaks with the voice of Athenian civic or political authority, comes to remind us that this, happily, is a play, and that its pattern must respect certain artistic canons; so, on Athena's authority, we are given a 'happy ending'. Athena confirms (1458–61) Iphigenia's judgement that divinity does not require human sacrifice. She signally declines (1438ff.) to explain why Apollo, after sending Orestes to Taurica, had not helped him to get safely away, or why Iphigenia's repeated prayers to Artemis had echoed in emptiness. Her reference to Poseidon sounds more like a confidential aside from the author than a part of the play.

Iphigenia's thoughts of Agamemnon lie even deeper than her thoughts of Artemis, and their intensity is reflected in the love of family and home which shows in all her words spoken to, or about, Orestes. 'My father sacrificed me . . .' It was forty-five years since the Elders of Argos in *Agamemnon* had described this scene, and the soothing formality which invests a legendary picture had spread its patina over Aeschylus' realism; but what Euripides confronts us with here is less 'the terror of the knife' (*Children of Heracles*, 562) which Macaria and Polyxena faced, than the violation of family love. This is shown by the sudden transition from a climax of indignation in 359–71 to the tenderness of 372–9. This play is full of memories of family occasions in Hellene homes. The family was the unit of loyalty and confidence on which the strength of every city was built. A number of Euripides' earlier plays arraigned the cruelty of fathers to their daughters (e.g., *Protesilaus*, *Cretan Women*, *Danaë*); this is the first of the complete plays to show in subtle detail the psychological effects of such cruelty: a noble nature perverted by ever-burning resentment. Iphigenia is 'a doomed victim of a father's villainy' (211), her life 'forfeit by her father's vow' (213); the saving of her life by Artemis had only transplanted her to a priesthood as hideous as the altar where she left her father. Her constant allusions to the family life she has lost are dominated by the rituals which family affection accords to death (159–66, 630–35).

When Orestes and Pylades stand before her, she sees their position as her own, pictures their family life, and pities their separation from it. Her questions lead soon to Aulis and her father's treachery. 'What of the successful general?' Then, when she hears he is dead, family love revives, and she weeps. News of the second crime against family love, Orestes' murder of his mother in the name of revenge, adds its confusion (559), to drown all censure in compassion; and speaking of her own death she says, 'She is to be pitied; so is he who killed his child?' This sudden liberation from resentment has a subtle consequence – her despondency changes in a flash to elation, so that on learning from the stranger that Orestes was alive a long time ago when he left Argos, she at once concludes, on no logical ground whatever, that her last night's dream was a lying message. After the recognition, however, joy prevails for only twenty-three lines (827–49), and then bitterness returns as Orestes reminds her that old crime does not die, in words which at last bring to the surface of ancient legend the agony and anxiety of the present day and the listening audience:

> Our house, our race, is noble; but the destiny
> That both our lives were born to, sister, is accursed.

The curse has come not by compulsion of events but by inexplicable choice, as Orestes had already stated (573-5):

> What galls one is that, while still of sound mind, he should,
> By heeding the words of prophets, plunge himself into
> A depth of ruin only experience can fathom.

The reminder of the curse recalls to Iphigenia what her father, while still of sound mind, had done to her; and for another twelve lines she dwells on the horror of Aulis.

Finally, when they begin to plot the theft of the image, Iphigenia tells Orestes (992-3), 'I wish now . . . to renounce bitterness against the hand that killed me'. She does not forget her father's act, for she speaks of it again in 1082; but her overcoming of resentment is shown by an adroit turn in 1187:

> Hellas destroyed me. I hate Hellas utterly.

This statement is essential to her deception of Thoas; and, because we know it is a deception, it is for us a statement that she has forgiven her father; and this means that she is ready to re-enter, and help to re-create, a family relationship of mutual love and trust.

Family love, however, is only one of life's relationships; Iphigenia shares her life with a group of Greek women, and the play shows what effect the betrayal of family love has had upon her social character. This appears first when she questions the unknown men about Hellene affairs (523-5):

> I too have an account to settle with Helen; and I
> am not alone – all Hellas hates her.

How does Iphigenia know this? She does not; but the more groundless hatred is, the more it insists on finding allies; and Orestes has hinted that he has no love for Helen. A few lines later comes Iphigenia's fervent thanksgiving for Calchas' death, and her no less fervent curse on Odysseus – both merited, no doubt; but we note that the first three people she asks about are people she hates; her hate is more impatient than her love. She asks next of Achilles, who had not wronged her; but her sole reaction to news of his death is to remember the treachery of which he was the tool. Then she asks for news of Agamemnon, and presses her request with the chilling phrase, 'It will give me pleasure to hear'. Chilling, because Orestes' first reply (546) has hinted at a sinister fate, and we wonder if the pleasure she showed on hearing bad news of Calchas will be repeated when she learns what happened to her father. On this occasion love defeats resentment, but we are soon shown that it does not extend beyond the family to friends.

When Iphigenia in the prologue first mourned for her brother's death, she needed the chorus to share her mourning, which they did. In their first stasimon the echo of Iphigenia's wishes goes side by side with their own bitter longing for home and freedom; and now, after listening to the sorrows of Iphigenia and Orestes, they suddenly ask to be included in the scene as human beings (576–7):

> And what of us? Do we not know what sorrow is?
> Our parents too were dear to us; where are they now?
> And living, or not living? Who can tell us this?

The first line of Iphigenia's reply seems to include them, but in the second we are disappointed – she is addressing only the two men. Then in her next two lines she speaks of a plan 'which will be welcome to everyone'; but what follows makes it plain that for Iphigenia 'everyone' includes herself and the man who can forward her family concerns, but not the chorus. After the recognition, in the brief moment of joy before dread again descends, Iphigenia calls on the chorus to share her happiness (842); but the plot for escape does not include the chorus, though she knows that their loyalty is essential. Euripides' plays are full of embarrassing moments, and this is a notable example. We can indeed sympathize with Iphigenia's intense longing for escape; but there is both in Orestes' words (1053–4) and in hers a note of calculation which grates unpleasantly; it could perhaps be there by chance, but it is more probable that the dramatist meant it to be felt. The one-sidedness of attitude shown in these expressions –

> Women have a feeling for one another . . .
> A single chance determines for three loving lives
> Between a safe homecoming and the stroke of death . . .
> I bid you think of the dear ones in your home – parents
> Or children . . .

though it may not move us to animosity against the speaker, shows us yet again the destructive effect of prolonged suffering. In the moment

before Athena arrives to close the real action we are shown first a
true selfless nobility which shames Iphigenia (1420–21), and then the
price of the chorus's loyalty (1431–3). It is curious that many modern
readers have seemed as unaware of this as Iphigenia is. That the poet
himself should be unaware of it, the nature of his whole work makes
incredible.

Iphigenia, then, is a complex character drawn in great detail. She
embodies, first, a comment on religion; secondly, a comment on the
family bond; thirdly, a comment on the effects of suffering. Above all
she is, in these three aspects, one of her author's clearest comments
on woman, who bears the major portion of the world's suffering,
whose constancy is the heart of home and family love, and whose
honourable place in religious ceremonial includes the function of
sacrificial victim.

The third theme in this play is the misery of exile and the sufferings
of severed families. Thucydides' account of the revolution in Corcyra
near the beginning of the war (III. 81–4) enables us to gauge the extent
to which the polarization of ideology corrupted the loyalty of blood,
dismembered families and destroyed homes, in cities large and small
in every district of Hellas, as long as the struggle continued. At the
time of this play the Sicilian expedition had caused a further dread, or
experience, of separation. Many, if not all, of the numerous cities
captured by either side in the last twenty years had endured in some
degree what the chorus describe in the second stasimon. 1106–22.
Whereas in *Electra* and *The Phoenician Women* the sorrows and pains of
exile are vividly depicted at relevant points, in this play the heart-
rending evocations of what life was like in Hellas 'before the war', in
lyrics and in iambics, spoken by Iphigenia and by the chorus, colour
the tone of the poem from beginning to end. The second stasimon in
particular claims for the chorus of captured Greek women the place
in general sympathy for which they begged Iphigenia in 576–7, only
to be ignored. Now they recall, not merely for Iphigenia's sake but
chiefly for their own, and so on behalf of every absent loved one re-
membered by each listener (1096–1105),

> . . . the festivals of Hellas,
> Where the people of my country gather;
> Longing for an Artemis whose worship is joy,

Who has her temple by the Cynthian hill
Where soft-haired palm and shapely laurel grow,
And the silver-green of the holy olive
Which sheltered Leto in her labour;
The round lake where water slowly turns,
Where the swan's chant honours the Muses.

Their fate had been not much less cruel than Iphigenia's; but Iphigenia will be carried home by an Argive galley, and will leave her friends behind, thinking of

The weddings in noble houses, the whirl of dancing,
The bridesmaids singing together, and I among them
In pride of youth and delicate ornament
And glory of rival graces;
When I would wear bright-coloured scarves
Which flowed with my long hair to shade my cheek!

The most tragic of the poets seldom touched more closely the source of immediate anguish in the lives of his audience.

This brings us to the fourth theme, the distinction between barbarian and Greek. The pathos of nostalgia is always sharpened by the blindness of absence. From prologue to epilogue this play presents the longing of captives, in a barbaric land dedicated to bloody rituals, for the innocent weddings and festivals of sunlit Hellas. And at every point the visitors' account of events in their beloved homeland poses the question: Is the difference as great as it is thought to be? The Athenian audience, familiar with the Orestes legend, accepted the matricide with the balanced judgement reflected by the 'even votes' of the traditional story. Whether rightly or wrongly, the Orestes of Aeschylus' *Choephori* and Sophocles' *Electra* was generally accepted as a blameless hero. Euripides both here and in *Electra* and *Orestes* condemned this calm acceptance and demanded a more sensitive judgement. When Iphigenia tells Thoas that the two men had killed their mother, the king's reply (1174),

Apollo! Even a savage would recoil from that!

probably made the audience laugh – at the notion that a crime had at last been discovered atrocious enough to shock a barbarian; but the audience's laughter makes the line the more pertinent. Modern readers have sometimes been more inclined to laugh with the Athenian majority than to reflect with the few; so that this sombre, intense, and ironic play has often been called a romantic escape-fantasy.

When Iphigenia in the prologue tells how she dreamt of home, she pictures first destruction, next the 'stranger-killing ritual' demanded of her in the barbaric temple (53). Soon after, she bemoans her exile, and in thinking of Hellas recalls 'the Argive Hymn to Hera' and the weaving of Pallas' robe by Athenian girls; contrasting these pleasures with the 'blood-streaming rites unfit for song' which accompany worship at the Taurian altar. Then the Herdsman brings his description of two unknown Greek gods on the shore – and a little later one of them is trembling, raging, slavering, and massacring cattle. When the men arrive, the chorus call them 'the pick of Hellene manhood' (459); and add that 'the law of Hellas declares such sacrifice abhorrent, unholy'. But before the first questioning is finished, Orestes has told of a husband murdered by his wife, a mother by her son, a daughter by her father; a guilty son exiled and homeless, and a world of gods 'as chaotic as our mortal world' (572). This is not the Hellas the chorus long for in 452–5 and 1137–51. This play, so far from inviting fantasy, begs its audience to fling away the fantasy of Hellenic moral superiority which, after twenty years of war, they still cling to, and to see themselves as they are. It is true that Orestes and Pylades show courage both on the shore and before the altar; but Orestes' madness has robbed him of hope: 'Our race is noble, but our destiny is accursed'. His hopelessness springs from guilt; but since he blames Apollo's command rather than his own obedience, he is as full of resentment as his sister. As a result, though he is not a vapid weakling like Orestes in Electra, nor a criminal lunatic as in Orestes, he is not to be unreservedly accepted as a hero.

So when Pylades says (905–6), 'Escape out of this savage place to safety'; when Iphigenia prays to Artemis, 'Graciously come with us out of this savage land to Athens; here is no fit place for your home, there a city of gladness awaits you'; and when Thoas undertakes (1482) to send the chorus home 'to Hellas blessed by Fortune'; it is possible that many of the audience whose thoughts ran in conventional grooves simply enjoyed a good story with a happy ending; but in 413 B.C. (just before the Sicilian disaster) or in 412 (just after it) the play had another message for some. The symbolism which in Orestes (408) connected the disasters of the House of Atreus with the waning fortunes of the Athenian state, and Orestes' insanity with her policy of war to the last gasp, was not yet worked out; but there are signs in this play that it was already conceived.

We come now to the central theme of all, the saga of the House of Atreus, and in particular the event which is the focus of the plot – the sacrifice of Iphigenia.

Six of the surviving plays of Euripides and one notable fragment (*Erechtheus*) deal with human sacrifice. In Aeschylus' *Agamemnon* the chorus, referring to the ritual at Aulis, do not say that it was a holy act divinely prescribed to further a war demanded by justice; they say it was an error of judgement on Agamemnon's part, committed 'to procure willing boldness in men who were going to their death' (*Agam.* 803–4). This subversive account of the matter attracted little notice, so far as we can tell, for forty-five years (*Agamemnon* was produced in 458); in the prologue of *Iphigenia in Tauris* the story is given its more usual religious colour. But Iphigenia's indignation in this play leaves little room for that pious submissiveness which is still – incredibly – accepted by many as a proper interpretation of the last scene of *Iphigenia at Aulis*; and implies what is there made explicit, that Aeschylus' Elders were right, and the murder was part of the commanders' expedient attempt to control a mutinous army. In *The Children of Heracles* (427) human sacrifice is prescribed, in dubious circumstances, to help a shifty king to evade his responsibility; and accepted by the victim in a contemptuous, triumphant gesture which forces him to fight in a just cause. In *Hecabe* the sacrifice of Polyxena is defended by Odysseus with an eloquent prevarication which points to a similar expediency; not even a god is cited as authority, merely the ghost of Achilles. In *Erechtheus* the speech of Praxithea offering her daughter for sacrifice is an ironic caricature of horrifying inhumanity and bogus patriotism. Polyxena's death is alluded to again in similar terms in *The Women of Troy*. In *The Phoenician Women* the prescription of human sacrifice is again made to appear both suspect and irrelevant; though Creon, by rejecting it, has incurred the censure of modern critics, who appear to regard Praxithea's attitude as more commendable.

What, then, was Euripides' purpose in returning so often to this theme, and what in particular is its significance in this play?

All Euripides' plays about sacrifice belong to the period of the Peloponnesian war. In each case the sacrifice is demanded for the sake of the victory or safe arrival of an army. The four victims most fully dealt with are women; Menoeceus in *The Phoenician Women* is an immature youth. In each case the connection, if any, between the ritual killing and the desired success is a matter of religious faith. In the two cases of Menoeceus and of Praxithea's daughter the victory which followed sacrifice was only less disastrous than total defeat. Macaria and Menoeceus are virtually forgotten as soon as they are out of sight. In *Hecabe* it is hinted – as in *Iphigenia at Aulis* it is made very clear – that the motive for ritual killing is the placating of a rabble of soldiers. In *Iphigenia in Tauris* the sacrifice apparently procured sailing-weather for the fleet, but engendered a curse which destroyed the royal house root and branch.

The metaphorical use of the word 'sacrifice' to denote the willing destruction of something valued, in the hope of gaining an end still more highly valued, is illustrated in *Orestes* 191, where Electra says that Apollo, in commanding her and her brother to commit matricide, 'sacrificed us utterly'. It seems a reasonable conclusion, from the facts reviewed in the last paragraph, that Euripides' plays about sacrifice are a part of his comment on the processes of war; touching, of course, on the obvious theme of the slaughter of young men, but pointing more directly at the miseries which war brings to women: the loss of status which increases, and often outlasts, the anguish of bereavement, the loneliness of wartime wives, the degradation and enslavement which can follow defeat; above all, the knowledge that, however full, varied, and secure her life might be – and Hellas provided many fifth-century women with a most enviable lot – it was always precarious. A husband's death, the demands of his business interests, his political activity, or mere change of affection, could at short notice leave her destitute and without any further prospect of a good life; and this insecurity was increased tenfold in time of war. Insecurity was of course shared by men; but the analogy of sacrifice points out that war is a male activity for the sake of which man claims the right to dispose at will the lives of women. We have seen this situation more gently pictured in *Alcestis*; in *Iphigenia* the harshness of it is fully voiced in the passionate words of the embittered victim.

This play, then, not only presents with some elaboration the two principal themes of Euripides' life's work, but illustrates at many points the power of his ironic method, the deep insight of his psychological portraiture, and his intense concern with living human issues. In addition to this, the poetic beauty of the lyrical portions, from the anguish of the first lament to the playfulness of the last stasimon, places this drama among the most satisfying and complete of the author's works.

ALCESTIS

CHARACTERS

APOLLO

DEATH

CHORUS, *citizens of Pherae in Thessaly*

FEMALE SERVANT

ALCESTIS, *wife of Admetus*

ADMETUS, *king of Pherae*

YOUNG SON *and* DAUGHTER *of Admetus*

HERACLES

PHERES, *father of Admetus*

MALE SERVANT

Scene: Before the palace of Admetus.

Enter APOLLO, *his bow slung over his shoulder,*
a quiver of arrows at his side.

APOLLO: House of Admetus! Here I have endured to live
Content with labourers' bread — yes, I, a god, Apollo.
Zeus was the cause; he killed my son Asclepius,
Struck him with lightning to the heart. And I was angry,
And killed the craftsmen of Zeus's fire, the Cyclopes.
For this my father made me serve a mortal man.
I came here, herdsman to a stranger. Till today
I have been this household's guardian. For here I found
Admetus, a good man, fit to entertain a god.
I saved his life; I gained — by cunning — the consent
Of the immortal Fates that this man should escape
Imminent death by offering to the powers below
Someone to die instead of him. So he went round
His family — tried them all, his father, his old mother;
And no one could he find willing to leave this light
And die for him, except his wife. So she now lies
Indoors, propped on their arms, and very near her end.
For she must die; this is the day the Fates have set
For her departure. And I too must leave this house,
Which I love dearly, to avoid the taint of death.

I see already Death himself, priest of the dead,
Coming. He has waited for this fateful day, and now
He is punctual. He will lead her to her home below.
                    Enter DEATH, *carrying a sword. On seeing*
                    APOLLO *he utters a cry of rage.*
DEATH: Phoebus! What are you doing here?
Why do you haunt this house? Have you come once more
To infringe, usurp, annul

The honours due to the powers below?
Were you not satisfied
When with a cunning trick you outwitted Fate
To cancel the death Admetus owed?
Now you are here again, waiting,
Armed with your bow, to save Alcestis too.
Yet this she undertook –
As the price of her husband's life, to forfeit hers.

APOLLO: Be calm; I have justice and good reason on my side.

DEATH: You have justice, you say: then what are your weapons for?

APOLLO: I have always made a habit of carrying this bow.

DEATH: Yes – and of showing unjust favours to this house.

APOLLO: I share the grief Admetus feels. He is my friend.

DEATH: So now you mean to rob me of a second life.

APOLLO: Remember, I did not take the first from you by force.

DEATH: How comes it, then, that he's above ground, not below?

APOLLO: He has given you his wife, whom you have come to fetch.

DEATH: And so I will; I'll take her down to the dead world.

APOLLO: Take her and go. I can't persuade you, I suppose –

DEATH: To do what? Kill those due to die? That is my work.

APOLLO: No, no; just to kill those who put off death too long.

DEATH: I take your drift. I know what you'd like me to do.

APOLLO: Some way, then, for Alcestis to live out her life?

DEATH: There is none. I, like others, value privilege.

APOLLO: You receive one life only, whether young or old.

DEATH: I gain a greater honour when the dead is young.

APOLLO: If she dies old, her grave will win a wealth of gifts.

DEATH: Phoebus, the law you formulate favours the rich.

APOLLO: You say so? Your wit has gone long unrecognized!

DEATH: For sale – to those who can afford it: ripe old age!

APOLLO: So you refuse to grant this favour that I ask?

DEATH: I do. You are acquainted with my principles.

APOLLO: I know them — hostile to mankind, abhorred by
   gods.

DEATH: You can't get everything you lawlessly desire.

APOLLO: I swear your harshness, though extreme, will meet
   its match.
   A man is on his way to Admetus' palace, who,
   Sent by Eurystheus to bring home from wintry Thrace
   A team of chariot-horses, will be welcomed here;
   And he will wrest Alcestis from your hand by force.
   And so you will perform all that I asked, and still
   Forfeit my gratitude and earn my enmity.

Exit APOLLO.

DEATH: Yes, you have words enough; no profit comes from
   words.
   This woman, then, shall come down to the house of Death.
   I'll go to find her, and with this sword solemnize
   The fatal rite. When once this sword has cut one lock
   Of hair, that soul is sacred to the nether gods.

DEATH *goes into the palace. Enter the* CHORUS,
from the town.

CHORUS: Why is everything so quiet
   Here at the palace? Why is there no sound?
   Not one friend of Admetus near to tell us
   Whether the queen, Alcestis, daughter of Pelias,
   Is dead, and we should mourn her,
   Or still lives in the light of day!
   In my belief, and in everyone's,
   She is the noblest wife a man ever had.

CHORUS A: Do you hear any sound in the house   *[Strophe*
   Of mourning[1] or of weeping?
   Or any cry to tell that all is over?

CHORUS B: Why, there is not even a house-slave
   Set to watch by the door.

Apollo, god of healing,
Appear now like a calm in stormy seas!

CHORUS A: There would not be this hush if she were dead.

CHORUS B: She must have died by now.

CHORUS A: At least they have not carried her out to burial.

CHORUS B: Why? I have little hope. What makes you sure?

CHORUS A: It is not possible that Admetus
Should bury his true and noble wife
Privately, without calling friends to mourn her.

CHORUS A: When someone has died, it is   [Antistrophe
customary
To place a bowl of spring-water before the door;
But I see none.

CHORUS B: And there would be a curl of hair
Cut for a sign of grief, and hung by the porch,
And the sound of young women wailing, if she were dead.

CHORUS A: And yet this surely was to be the day –

CHORUS B: The day?

CHORUS A: When she must pass to the world below?

CHORUS B: You have touched my heart; you have touched
my thought.

CHORUS A: A noble life is worn to the last thread;
And a man must grieve whose heart
The years have taught to be true.

CHORUS: Even if a ship were dispatched to Lycia   [Strophe
Or to the temple of Ammon in the waterless desert,
No help could be found either there or anywhere
To ransom the doomed queen's life.
Death, abrupt and absolute, is close at hand.
To what altar of gods, to what priest
Should I go with sheep for sacrifice?
I know of none.

Yes, there was one: [Antistrophe
If only Asclepius, son of Apollo,

Still saw this light with living eyes,
Alcestis would come back, leaving behind her
The dark underworld and the doors of death.
For he raised up the dead, until he himself
Died from the stroke of a fiery thunderbolt
Flung by the hand of Zeus.
And now, where can we turn for hope?

The king has left no pious act undone,
No prayer unsaid; on every altar
Blood streams in sacrifice; yet anguish finds no cure.

Enter a FEMALE SERVANT *of* ALCESTIS.

CHORUS: Look, here's a servant coming out, and full of tears.
   What will she tell us? — My good woman, it is natural
   That you should feel distressed over your master's grief.
   But tell us: does his wife still live? or has she died?
SERVANT: She lives; but it would be as true to say she's dead.
CHORUS: But the same person cannot be alive and dead.
SERVANT: She can't hold herself upright now; she gasps for
   breath.
CHORUS: Poor man! So good a husband! What a wife to lose!
SERVANT: He does not know how good she is; but suffering
   Will teach him.
CHORUS: Is there no more hope of saving her?
SERVANT: No more. This is the appointed day; time will not
   wait.
CHORUS: The ceremonial preparations are in hand?
SERVANT: Her robe and jewels are ready for her burial.
CHORUS: Let her be sure of this: her death will make her
   famous
   As the most noble of all women in the wide earth.
SERVANT: Truly she is the noblest; who can question that?
   What must the woman be who could surpass her? How
   Could any wife give clearer testimony that she
   Honours her husband, than by freely dying for him?

This the whole city knows; but it will touch your heart
To hear how she has spent these last hours in her home.

She knew that her appointed day had come. So first
She washed her white body in water from the stream;
Next, from her store-room lined with cedar-wood she took
A gown and jewels, and dressed herself becomingly;
Then stood before the altar of Hestia, and prayed:
'Goddess, since I am going below the earth, I now
Pay my last worship to you. Watch over my children,
I beseech you; let my son wed with a loving wife,
My daughter with a noble husband. Let them not
Be cut off like their mother, to die before their time.
Give them good fortune, and a long and happy life
In their own country.'

                        Then she went to every altar
In the whole palace, and before praying decked each one
With garlands of green myrtle she had picked herself.
No tear fell, not a sigh was heard. Her lovely face
Did not change colour, gave no sign of what must come.
Then, to her room; and now indeed, flinging herself
Down on the bed, she wept. 'O marriage-bed,' she cried,
'Farewell! Here once I gave my maidenhood to him;
And now my life. I do not hate you; yet you have
Killed me, for I alone[2] would not be false to you
And to my husband; and for this I die. So now
Some other woman will possess you; she may be
More fortunate, but not a truer, better wife.'

Kneeling beside her bed, she kissed it; and the tears
Streamed from her eyes till the whole coverlet was wet.
At last, when she could not weep any more, she wrenched
Herself away, and went out, stumbling helplessly.
Then back – away again – and many times she turned
And then returned to throw herself yet once again
Upon her bed. Her children, clinging to her dress,
Wept too; she clasped them each in turn, and said farewell,

And told them she must die, and kissed them. Everywhere
The servants, broken-hearted, were all weeping. She
Took each one by the hand, and spoke to each, and each
To her, even the humblest. So, Admetus' house
Is full of trouble. Had he died, what then? He would
Have died. But he escaped; and he possesses now
A memory that will be a lifelong agony.

CHORUS: Surely Admetus feels the most acute distress
At being deprived perforce of such a noble wife?

SERVANT: Oh, yes, he weeps, and clasps his dear wife in his
arms,
Beseeching her not to desert him.[3] But he asks
The impossible; her sickness drains the life away.
Her helplessness is pitiable; she lies, a limp
Weight in his arms. Yet, though her breath is failing, still
She wants to take one final look, her last of all,
At the bright sunlight. I will go in and tell her now
That you have come. It is not everyone who loves
My master enough to stand beside him loyally
In trouble; but you have been his friend for a long time.

Exit to palace.

CHORUS (*speaking severally*):
— Listen, Zeus! Where is there —   [*Strophe*
What way out is there, what solution
Of this predicament that confronts the king?
— Will someone come? Or is it time
Already for the shorn head
And the black cloak wrapped around for grief?
— The truth is clear, friends, quite clear.
Nevertheless let us pray to the gods;
The power of gods is very great.
— Apollo, lord of healing,
Seek out some remedy for Admetus;
Send now, send help. As before you found a way,
So appear again, a deliverer from death,

And quell the cruelty of the grave.

– It is a terrible thing that you suffer,   [*Antistrophe*
Son of Pheres, in the loss of your wife.
– Well might a man so afflicted
Quench his own breath with sword or swinging noose;
For he this very day shall see his wife,
Dear beyond telling, dearer than all, dead.
– Look! The doors open; here she comes,
And her husband with her.
– Lament, my land and city,
Weep for the noble wife who goes,
Wasting with sickness,
Down to the deep earth and the house of death.

CHORUS: That the joys of marriage outweigh its pain
    I shall always deny, judging from past experience,
    And seeing where Admetus stands today.
    When he has lost his loyal Alcestis,
    His life thereafter will be not worth living.[4]
    ALCESTIS, *supported by* ADMETUS, *comes from the palace;*
        with her, the little boy EUMELUS *and his sister.*
        ALCESTIS *is at first in a sort of trance.*
ALCESTIS: O Sun! O light of the day!
    O heavenward eddies of the scudding cloud!
ADMETUS: The sun can see that you and I, who suffer thus,
    Have done the gods no wrong which could deserve your
        death.
ALCESTIS: O earth, and the walls of home!
    And Iolcos, that sheltered my birth and childhood!
ADMETUS: Lift yourself up; do not give in, but pray.
    The gods are powerful, and may yet be merciful.
ALCESTIS: I see the two-oared boat coming over the lake;
    And Charon, ferryman of the dead,
    Leans on his pole, and already calls me:

'Why are you so slow? Hurry; you make me late!'
You hear? He is urging me impatiently.

ADMETUS: It stabs my heart to hear you speak of Charon and
That dark crossing. O gods! Why must we suffer so?

ALCESTIS: I feel a hand grasping my hand,
Leading me — don't you see him? — leading me
To the home of the dead. He has wings;
His eyes glow dark under his frowning brow.
[*To* ADMETUS, *who clasps her*] What are you doing? Let me
go.
I am treading a fearful path; I am terrified.

ADMETUS: And we who love you are heartbroken; most of all
I and these children whose distress is shared with me.

ALCESTIS *now speaks to those around her; the trance is over.*

ALCESTIS: Let me go now; take away your hands.
Lay me down; I have no strength to stand.
Death is near.
The darkness of night creeps over my eyes.
Children, my children, you have a mother no more,
No more. Good-bye! Dear children,
May you be happy in living!

ADMETUS: No, not 'good-bye'! This bitter word
Is to me worse than any death.
Have you the heart to abandon me?
In the gods' name, for the sake of these children
Whom you will leave motherless,
Rise up, take courage!
I cannot live when you are dead;
For me, living and dying are in you alone;
Your love demands my worship!

ALCESTIS: Admetus, you see how things go with me; I want,
Before I die, to tell you what my wishes are.
Because I put you first, because I was resolved
That you should keep your life at cost of mine, I now
Am dying in your place; though I need not have died.

I could have married any Thessalian I chose,
And ruled a palace, rich and royal. But to live
Parted from you, and these children unfathered – that
I would not bear. My youth, filled with delight and joy,
I gave up. Yet your father and your mother, who
Were of an age to die honoured by everyone,
And could have saved their son and gained a glorious death –
They failed you. You were their one son; they had no hope,
When you were dead, that others could be born to them.
Both you and I could then have lived our length of years;
You would not have to mourn your wife in loneliness
And bring up children with no mother. But all this
Some god has ordained for us, to be as it is.

Your part, then, is to remember what I did for you.
And I ask now, not for a gift of equal cost,
Since there is no gift costlier than life; but you
Will call it just, for you are a good man, and love
These two children not less than I do: keep them, then,
Inheritors of my house, give them no stepmother
To envy my royal birth and vent her jealousy
In harsh oppression of these children, yours and mine.
I beg you, Admetus, do not do this. A stepmother
Comes in like an enemy to children – yes, an adder
Is not more cruel. A boy, now, has a tower of strength
In his own father; but, dear daughter, how will you
Find happiness as you grow up to womanhood?
What will your father's wife be to you? Might she not
Put evil slanders on you in your flower of youth
And blight your marriage? Your own mother never will
Arrange your bridal veil, be there to hold your hand
In childbirth, when her comfort is your deepest need.
I must die. It is not tomorrow that this debt
Falls due, nor after two days' grace; this very hour
I shall be spoken of as a woman who once lived.

Good-bye! Be happy! You, my husband, may be proud

To know you married a good wife; and you, dear children,
Remember too that you were born of a good mother.

CHORUS: You need not fear; I am ready to answer for
   Admetus.

He is a good man;[5] he will carry out your wish.

ADMETUS: I will, I will! Have no fear. While you lived you
   were

My wife; and dying you alone will bear that name.
And no Thessalian bride shall ever take your place,
To call me husband; there is none so royal in birth,
Of such rare beauty, that could win me. I am content
With these two children, and pray the gods to give me joy
In them, since I have lost the joy I had in you.

And not for one year only, Alcestis, but as long
As my life lasts, I shall endure my grief for you,
Counting my mother and my father as enemies,
Hating them; for they loved me in word but not in deed.
But you, by bartering your own precious life for mine,
Saved me. Shall I not mourn, when I am losing you –
So rare a wife? There shall be no more dancing here;
The crowded feasts, the merrymaking that filled this house,
The garlands, music – all that is finished. I could never
Finger my lyre again, or rouse my heart to sing
To the Libyan flute. My life's delights vanish with you.

I shall bid a cunning sculptor carve your image in stone,
And it shall lie stretched on our bed, and I shall kneel
Beside it, and throw my arms round it, and speak your name,
And vainly think I hold my dear wife in my arms –
Cold comfort, truly; none the less, a way to lighten
My heavy heart. Then in my dreams you'd come and go,
Making me glad; to see a loved face even in dreams
Brings pleasure, for as long as the illusion lasts.

Oh, if I had the songs that Orpheus had, his voice,
To enchant with music Pluto and Persephone,
I would go down to fetch you; and not Cerberus

Would stop me – no, nor Charon's ferry-load of ghosts,
Till I had brought you living to the light of day! –
It cannot be. Look for me there when I shall die;
And make a home ready, where you can be with me.
I shall command these children to entomb us both
In one coffin of cedar-wood, and to lay out
My body close to yours. I will not, even in death,
Be parted from you, who alone are true to me.

CHORUS: Admetus, I will share with you this sharp sorrow
As friend with friend. Alcestis is worth all your tears.

ALCESTIS: My children, you have heard for yourselves your
father's words.
His promise is, he will not take another wife
Or give you a second mother, but will honour me.

ADMETUS: I now renew my promise, and will keep my word.

ALCESTIS: For that promise, receive these children from my
hand.

ADMETUS: I take them, so; a dear gift from your hand, dear
wife.

ALCESTIS: You must now be a mother to them in my place.

ADMETUS: It is my bounden duty; they will feel your loss.

ALCESTIS: When you most need me living, children, I must
die.

ADMETUS: What shall I do when you have left me solitary?

ALCESTIS: One who is dead is nothing. Time will soften pain.

ADMETUS: Oh, take me with you, in the gods' name take me
too!

ALCESTIS: It is for you I am going; one death is enough.

ADMETUS: O Fate! How noble is the wife you take from
me!

ALCESTIS: Darkness and heaviness drop down over my eyes.

ADMETUS: My life is ended, if you are truly leaving me.

ALCESTIS: To speak truly, say I am no one now, nothing.

ADMETUS: Look up! These are your children; don't abandon
them.

ALCESTIS: I do not want to leave them, but – good-bye, children.

ADMETUS: Look at them, look at them!

ALCESTIS: I am already gone.

ADMETUS: What is it? Are you faint?

ALCESTIS: Good-bye.

ADMETUS: This ends my life.

CHORUS: Admetus' wife is gone, Alcestis is no more.

EUMELUS: What shall I do? My mother has left us, father.
    She lives no more in the sun;
    She has left me to a desolate life.
    Look – look at her eyes and her limp hands.
    Mother! Listen, I beg you, listen to me.
    It is I, mother, kneeling by your pillow;
    It is your little child, calling you with kisses!

ADMETUS: She cannot hear or see you when you speak to her.
    Children, this blow is more than I or you can bear.

EUMELUS: I am young to walk alone,
    Left without my mother.
    This loss will bring me bitter troubles
    Which you, my sister, you must share.
    Father, you had no joy of your marriage, none;
    She perished first, and could not come with you
    To the limit of old age.
    With her departing our whole house is dead.

CHORUS: Her death, Admetus, is a blow which you must bear.
    You are not the first of mortal men – no, nor the last –
    To lose a noble-hearted wife. Consider this:
    Death is a debt which every one of us must pay.

ADMETUS: I know it; and this trouble fell not suddenly
    Or unexpected. The foreknowledge of this day
    Has for a long time tortured me. But now I must
    Order Alcestis' funeral rites. Stay with us, then,
    And join our hymn to the implacable god of death.

I command every Thessalian under my rule
To do his part in ritual mourning for the queen,
And wear the shorn head and the sombre funeral dress.
You who yoke four-horse chariots, and all riders,
Crop short your horses' manes. Throughout the whole city
Let no music of flute or string be heard till twelve
Full months are past. Never shall I commit to earth
One more beloved, more loyal to me. I owe to her
All honour; for she alone has given her life for mine.

Servants now carry the body of ALCESTIS *into the palace.*
ADMETUS *follows.*

CHORUS: Daughter of Pelias, may peace go with   [*Strophe*
      you
   As in the palace of Death
   You enter your sunless home.
   Let the black-haired god of the deep earth know her;
   Let the ghostly ferryman,
   Ancient Charon, bent over oar and rudder,
   Know that his craft has carried across stagnant Acheron
   One alone the noblest of all women.

   Many a song shall poets make,   [*Antistrophe*
   Singing your praise to the seven-stringed mountain lyre,
   Or in unaccompanied chorus,
   When in Sparta the circling season
   Brings round the month of the Carneian feast
   And the lofty moon beams all night;
   Or in the splendid streets of shining Athens.
   Such a theme for music
   Your death has bequeathed to singers.

   Would that it lay within my choice or power   [*Strophe*
   To bring you back to the day's light
   Out of the house of death,

Up from the river of weeping,
To reverse your passage[6] over the dark waters!
For you, most belov'd of women, you alone
Fearlessly surrendered your life
To ransom your husband from the grave.
Lightly fall the earth above you, Alcestis!
And should your husband marry a second time,
Then in truth, to me and to your children,
He would be a man abhorred.

His mother would not consent,   [*Antistrophe*
For her son's sake, to hide her flesh in the earth;
His father too refused[7] . . . A wretched pair,
Both lacked courage to rescue their own son,
Though both were grey-headed.
But you in the flower of your youth
Have taken Admetus' place, and now are dead.
May it be my fortune to find in a wedded wife
Love of such quality – in this world a rare occurrence;
But I know that, to me, such a partner
Would bring perpetual content.

    Enter HERACLES; *the* CHORUS *recognize him by his*
            lion-skin cloak and his club.

HERACLES: Good friends, who live in this Pheraean country-
    side,
   Is it my luck to find Admetus here at home?
CHORUS: Why, yes, Admetus is indoors now, Heracles.
   But tell us, what need sends you here to Thessaly?
   And why does Pherae draw you to its walls and streets?
HERACLES: Eurystheus king of Tiryns has set me a task.
CHORUS: Where must you go? What distant journey is
    forced on you?
HERACLES: To Thrace, to bring back Diomede's team of
    four wild mares.

CHORUS: How can you do that? No doubt you know Diomede?

HERACLES: I do not know him. I was never before in Thrace.

CHORUS: You'll not be master of those mares without a fight.

HERACLES: Nor is it possible to refuse what's laid on me.

CHORUS: Kill Diomede and come back – or get killed and stay there!

HERACLES: This will not be the first time that I've staked my life.

CHORUS: Even when you've overcome him, what can you do then?

HERACLES: I shall bring back his horses to the king of Tiryns.

CHORUS: No easy matter to fasten bridles on those jaws.

HERACLES: I'll do it, if their nostrils don't snort fire at me.

CHORUS: Why, they attack men with their teeth and chew them up!

HERACLES: That's not what horses feed on; only bears and wolves.

CHORUS: You'll see – their very mangers are bedaubed with blood.

HERACLES: The man who bred them – whose son is he said to be?

CHORUS: The son of Ares, lord of the golden Thracian shield.

HERACLES: You are right; and this task too matches my destiny,
   A rocky, uphill road right to the end. I must
   Fight every son that Ares fathered; first Lycaon,
   Then Cycnus; now I'm going to challenge Diomede
   And his horses. Well, I am Alcmene's son: no man
   Shall ever see me tremble at an enemy's strength.

CHORUS: But look! The king himself is coming from the palace.
   Enter ADMETUS, *with his hair cut in sign of mourning;*
      a servant attends him.

ADMETUS: Heracles! Son of Zeus, grandson of Perseus, welcome!

HERACLES: All happiness to you, Admetus, king of Thessaly!

ADMETUS: So I could wish. I know your thought for me is kind.

HERACLES: But what's the cause of this funereal short hair?

ADMETUS: A death. I have a burial to perform today.

HERACLES: You have not lost one of your children? Heaven forbid!

ADMETUS: No, no; my children are indoors, alive and well.

HERACLES: I take it, then – your father – ? He was a ripe age.

ADMETUS: My father and my mother both live, Heracles.

HERACLES: Why, surely it's not your wife Alcestis who has died?

ADMETUS: There are two answers I could give you about her.

HERACLES: Well, do you mean she's dead, or is she still alive?

ADMETUS: She is, and is no more; and this distresses me.

HERACLES: I am still no wiser. What you say mystifies me.

ADMETUS: Do you not know what is fated to become of her?

HERACLES: I know she undertook to die instead of you.

ADMETUS: That once agreed, how can I say she is still alive?

HERACLES: Heavens, man! Don't start weeping for your wife so soon!
  Put that off till the time comes.

ADMETUS: One who is due to die
  Is dead already; and the dead are nothing now.

HERACLES: Most people see a difference between alive and dead.

ADMETUS: You think in one way, Heracles, I in another.

HERACLES: Well, now – this friend you're mourning for: who was the man?

ADMETUS: The woman. It was a woman I alluded to.

HERACLES: A blood-relation? Or of another family?

ADMETUS: A dear friend of our household, but no relative.

HERACLES: How did it happen that she died here in your house?

ADMETUS: She came here to live with us when her father died.

HERACLES [*preparing to go*]: Ah, well;
  I wish I had come, Admetus, when you were not in mourning.

ADMETUS: Why, what do you mean? Where are you going, Heracles?

HERACLES: I must go on now. I'll stay with some other friend.

ADMETUS: My lord, you cannot! I will not hear of such a thing.

HERACLES: No guest is welcome on the day of a funeral.

ADMETUS: Those who have died are dead. Now, come into my house.

HERACLES: It's all wrong for a guest to feast while his host mourns.

ADMETUS: The guest-rooms are quite separate. We will take you there.

HERACLES: Let me go; I shall still be deeply in your debt.[8]

ADMETUS: I cannot let you go to stay with another man.
  [*To the Servant*] You! Show our visitor the way, and open up
  The outer guest-rooms. Tell the stewards in charge to see
  That food's provided in abundance; and take care
  To shut the courtyard doors. I do not want our guest
  At table to have his pleasure spoilt by sounds of grief.

    HERACLES *goes into the palace, followed by the Servant.*

CHORUS: What are you doing, Admetus? At a time like this
  Have you the heart to welcome guests? What folly is this?

ADMETUS: He came to me as a guest. If I had turned him from
  My house, or from my city, would you have praised me more?
  Far from it; that could not have made my circumstance
  Less painful; I'd have been guilty of discourtesy;
  And to our present pain a further pain would be
  Added, that my house should be called inhospitable.

And Heracles is always a good friend to me
When I go travelling on those thirsty Argive roads.

CHORUS: But why, then, did you hide from him the present case,
If, as you say yourself, your guest was an old friend?

ADMETUS: He never would have agreed to set foot in the house
If he had known the truth of what has happened to me.
Well, some, no doubt, will think me a fool for acting thus,
And criticize me; but my house has yet to learn
Such conduct as to shut the door in a friend's face.

Exit ADMETUS *to the palace.*

CHORUS: House of unfailing welcome,   [*Strophe*
House of the generous host!
Under your roof Apollo chose to live,
The prophet, the musician;
And as a member of your household
Was content to graze your sheep,
Piping a tune of shepherd's love
Over the steep winding pastures.

Spotted lynxes loved his music and came   [*Antistrophe*
To feed beside his flock,
And a tawny herd of lions
Came from the glen of Othrys;
And around your lute, Apollo,
Dappled fawns, stepping out
Slender-footed from the high shady fir-trees,
Danced for joy to your enchanting notes.

Thus through divine protection   [*Strophe*
Admetus' hearth and lands surpass in wealth all others
That live beside the pleasant Boebian lake.
Westward, his ploughed acres and level pastures
Stretch on to where the sun

Stables his horses under the dark Molossian sky;
While seaward, to the east, Mount Pelion,
On the rock-bound Aegean coast, is his domain.

Now again he has thrown wide his door   [*Antistrophe*
And welcomed a guest, while his own eyes held tears
Of lament for the still warm flesh
Of a wife dead in his house; for the kingly mind
Honours to excess the duties of friendship.
Yet in such excess, when intent is honest,
Lies full wisdom. This to me is a marvel;
But confidence sits firm in my heart
That one who fears the gods will prosper well.

Enter ADMETUS, *with attendants bearing the body of* ALCESTIS.

ADMETUS: Your presence here, Pheraeans, shows your
    friendly hearts.
Everything now is ready; and Alcestis comes
Carried by servants shoulder-high to burial.[9]
As she goes out on her last journey, will you, Elders,
Pronounce for her the farewell that is customary?

CHORUS: Admetus, look! I see your aged father coming
On foot, and there are servants with him, carrying
His funeral gifts, a robe and jewels for your wife.

Enter PHERES, *attended.*

PHERES: My son, I have come to sympathize with your distress.
You have lost, beyond all doubt, a noble, modest wife.
Such loss is painful to endure; and yet we must
Endure it. Now, accept these gifts, let them be buried
With her. It is our duty to honour her remains;
For she has rendered up her life for yours, my son.
She would not see me childless, let me waste away
Into a miserable old age, deprived of you.
By her courageous, noble sacrifice she gives
New dignity of life to the whole female sex.
Farewell, Alcestis! You have saved my son, and raised

Me from the grave. Peace be with you, even in the house
Of death! [To ADMETUS] You know, with a woman like
    that, a man can find
That marriage pays; otherwise, it's a bad bargain.
ADMETUS: I did not invite you to attend this funeral.
You are not here as one of my friends; nor shall she
Ever wear any gift of yours. Her grave will be,
Without your contribution, furnished honourably.
When I was dying — that was the time for you to show
Sympathy. Then you stood back; you let another die,
Though she was young and you were old. And now you come
To howl over her corpse! You're no true father of mine![10]
You have been put to the test, and shown your true colours;
And I refuse to be called your son. You surely must
Be unsurpassed in cowardice; aged as you are,
Having reached the very limit of life, you had neither will
Nor courage to face death for your son's sake. Instead
You yielded place to her — a woman from another city.
It is she, and no one else, that I should rightly call
Both mother and father. Think what glory you would have
    gained
By dying for your own son, when in any case you had
Only a short time left to live. You had already
Enjoyed all that a man requires for happiness:
You became king in your prime of youth; you had a son
To succeed to this estate, so that your house would not
Be left without inheritor to the rapacity
Of strangers. And you will hardly say it was because
I dishonoured your grey hairs that you abandoned me
To death — when I have always given first duty and love
To you. And with what gratitude you and my mother
Repaid me! I tell you, you had best lose no more time
In breeding sons to care for your old age, and when
You die, to shroud your body and carry it to the grave.
I shall not lift a hand to bury you; I am dead,

For all you care. If I, through another's act of love,
Still see the light of the sun, then to that other I owe
My filial love and duty. I have heard old men
Praying for death, cursing the long slow senile years:
Hypocrites! When death comes in sight, not one of them
Has a mind to die; old age has lost its bitterness.

CHORUS: Stop, both of you! Our present trouble is enough.
Admetus, don't provoke your father's rage too far.

PHERES: And who do you think you are reviling, insolent
boy?
Some wretched Lydian slave bought with your own money?
I am a Thessalian; so was my father. We
Are pure-bred and free-born, and well you know it, boy.
You go too far, flinging these wild insults. Face me!
You shall not turn your back before I've answered you.
    I am your father, and I reared you to inherit
My house; but I've no obligation to die for you.
There exists no such tradition in our family,
Nor anywhere in Hellas, that fathers die for sons.
Good luck or bad luck, your life is your own concern.
I have done my duty by you; you have wide possessions;
The large estate which I inherited I shall leave
To you. How have I wronged you? What do I rob you of?
Don't you die for your father, and I'll not die for you.
You enjoy life: do you think I don't enjoy it too?
By my reckoning, I'm going to spend a long time dead
And a short time alive – yes, short, but very sweet.
You certainly took pains enough to evade death,
And without a blush; you have lived past your appointed
time,
And you've killed her – and then, you blackguard, you call
me
A coward! – you, with less courage than your own wife,
Who died to save her young, heroic husband – you!
    You are ingenious too; you have found out a way

Never to die at all — get each successive wife
To die for you! How dare you, being a coward yourself,
Abuse a relative who's reluctant to oblige?
Now hold your tongue, and think this over: if you love
Your life, why, so does every man; and your insults
To me will be repaid with interest — and with truth!

CHORUS: You have both in turn abused each other more than
enough.

Come, Pheres, calm this violent rage against your son.

ADMETUS: Talk on; I have said all I want to. If the truth
Hurts you, it is your doing. You are in the wrong.

PHERES: And still more wrong I should have been, to die for
you.

ADMETUS: Dying is different for an old man. I am young.

PHERES: We owe our one life to ourselves. We can't live
two.[11]

ADMETUS: Why, then, I hope you live a longer span than
Zeus!

PHERES: You curse your father? What wrong have I done to
you?

ADMETUS: I understood you were in love with a long life.

PHERES: I? What of you? You're burying her in your own
place!

ADMETUS: Her tomb is a memorial to your cowardice.

PHERES: At least I didn't kill her — you dare not say that.

ADMETUS: Oh! How I hope that you one day will need my
help.

PHERES: Marry wife after wife, let them all die for you!

ADMETUS: And so they would; but you refused — more shame
to you.

PHERES: The sun-god gives us light; and it is sweet, yes,
sweet.

ADMETUS: Whimpering weakness! Do you call yourself a
man?

PHERES: You laugh; but it's not *my* old corpse you're burying.

ADMETUS: When *you* go to your grave there'll be no praises sung.

PHERES: Little I care who speaks ill of me – in my grave.

ADMETUS: Hear that! What sense of honour does an old man have?

PHERES: Well, *she* had honour – but no sense, as you found out.

ADMETUS: Will you go home? Leave me to bury her in peace.

PHERES: I'll go. You murdered her, and you shall bury her;
But you'll be brought to book yet by her family.
Yes! If Acastus is the man he used to be
He'll make you pay the fair price for his sister's blood!

Exit, while ADMETUS *shouts after him.*

ADMETUS: Get out of my sight, both you and the woman you keep!
Grow old childless as you deserve, though your son lives;
And never come under one roof with me again! –
If it were lawful to proclaim publicly that I
Renounce a son's right in my father's hearth and home,
I would have done so.

*There is a pause. The coffin still waits at
the centre of the stage.*

Now, friends, we have before us a sad task, and must
Perform it. Let us go to lay her in her grave.[12]

CHORUS: Farewell, Alcestis;
Farewell, unflinching in courage,
Great-hearted, first in faithfulness!
Hermes and the dread King
Give you kind welcome to the earthy shades!
If there high place is kept
For noble spirits, may you
Receive full honour, throned beside Persephone!

The CHORUS *join the funeral procession and exeunt. As their music
recedes, a different music, a drunken bawling, mingles audibly with it.
The* SERVANT *who was ordered to attend* HERACLES *then enters.*

SERVANT: I have seen guests in plenty, from all sorts of places,
   Come to this house; and I've served them at dinner; but
   I've never yet made welcome a worse guest than this.
   To start with, he could see my master was in mourning;
   He never ought to have crossed the step; yet – in he walks.
   Next, at the table – since he knows our circumstances,
   Does he politely take what's put in front of him?
   Not a bit! Anything we don't bring, he shouts at us
   To fetch. He takes the ivy-wood cup in both hands
   And tosses off the blessed liquor – neat! And soon
   The drink goes to his brain, begins to warm him up.
   He winds a wreath of myrtle-leaves around his head,
   And starts a hideous bawling. Well, there were two tunes
   Going on together: he was singing, without a thought
   For the sorrow in this house; while in the servants' room
   We were all weeping for our mistress. But we took care
   Not to look straight at him with tears filling our eyes –
   The king gave orders about this. Now, here I am
   Indoors, serving a guest – some rascally thief or bandit;
   While she, Alcestis, has gone out of the house; and I
   Did not follow her body, or even stretch my hand
   To say good-bye, nor join in the lament for her.
   To me and to all the servants here she was a mother.
   A thousand times, when the king was raging, it was she
   Who calmed him down and saved us. So, this guest who
     comes
   Bursting in on our trouble – I hate him; and I'm right!
              Enter HERACLES.
HERACLES: Here, you! Why do you look so solemn? What
   are you
   Cogitating about? A servant ought not to stand
   Scowling at a guest; you should receive him affably.
   Instead, you see before you an old friend of your master's,
   And you stand glowering at him as if you hated him –
   And why? Because some stranger has died, and you're upset!

Now, you're a wise man; come here, and grow wiser still.
Friend, dost thou understand[13] the nature of mortal life?
I think not. Who would have told you? Well now, listen
   to me.
All mortal men are bound to die – inevitably.
There's no man living who can confidently say –
Not one – that he will still be living the next day.
The road of chance leads on by a mysterious way;[14]
It can't be taught, nor is it grasped by human skill.
So, now you've heard and profited from what I've said;
Well, then, cheer up, and drink! Say to yourself, 'Today
My life's my own; tomorrow it belongs to Fortune.'
   And there's another goddess too that you must honour:
The most delightful, charming Aphrodite. She
Is a sweet, lovely goddess. All these other cares
And griefs – forget them; just do as I say, if you
Agree that my advice is good – I think you do.
   Come on! Away with this excessive melancholy;
Rise above circumstances; put a garland on
Your head; and join me in a cup of wine. The cure[15]
For gloomy thoughts and knotted brows is the sweet splash
Of wine in a wine-cup – I'm sure of it. You know,
We're mortals, you and I; we should behave like mortals.
As for these solemn souls, these anxious worriers,
If you want my opinion, life for all that kind
Isn't life at all; it's just one long calamity!

SERVANT: Yes, I know all this. But today we are not disposed
   To merrymaking. We have other things to do.

HERACLES: The dead woman was not of this family. Don't
   take it
So much to heart. Your master and mistress are both well.

SERVANT: What? Well, you say? Do you not know what has
   happened here?

HERACLES: Why, yes, I know; unless your master told me
   lies.

SERVANT: He carries hospitality too far, much too far.

HERACLES: Must I be turned away for a stranger's funeral?

SERVANT: Stranger – oh, yes; a total stranger to us all!

HERACLES: Is there some serious trouble he has kept from me?

SERVANT: No more now, please. Our master's trouble is our concern.

HERACLES: This points to something other than a stranger's death.

SERVANT: It does; or why should I be upset at seeing you Enjoy yourself?

HERACLES: Why should my friend treat me like this?

SERVANT: You came at a time when it was wrong to welcome you.
The household is in mourning. We're all wearing black,
As you can see; our heads are shorn.

HERACLES: But who has died?
One of Admetus' children? Or his father, then?

SERVANT: No, no. It is his wife, Alcestis, who has died.

HERACLES: His wife is dead? And you received me as a guest?

SERVANT: He was too honourable to turn you from the door.

HERACLES: Poor man! What suffering, to lose so noble a wife!

SERVANT: Not *her* life only; all our lives, we feel, are lost.

HERACLES: I saw his tears, and felt that grief lay deep under
The outward signs. He spoke of a stranger's funeral;
And I believed him, and blundered in, reluctantly,
To abuse the hospitality of a bereaved friend
With wine and feasting, and a garland on my head!
And you – when such a thing had happened, to say nothing!
I'm going. Where shall I find them? Where's he burying her?

SERVANT: As you leave the city, on the straight road to Larissa,
You will see before you a tomb of polished stone.

Exit SERVANT.

HERACLES: Come now, my endlessly enduring heart and hand,
Now show what sort of son Alcmene of Tiryns bore

To immortal Zeus! The woman's newly dead; and I
Must save her, and pay my debt of kindness to Admetus,
Setting Alcestis safe again in her own home.
The black-robed king of the dead will come to drink the
    blood
Of victims offered at her tomb. I'll go there, hide,
And watch for him, and so leap out and spring on him.
And once I have my arms locked round his writhing ribs,
There is no power that can release him, till he yields
Alcestis to me. And if I miss my prey this time,
If Death does not come to the bait of blood, I'll go
Down to the sunless palace of Persephone
And Pluto, and I'll ask for her. And, by my soul,
I'll bring Alcestis up again, and deliver her
Into Admetus' hands – my true friend, who would not,
Even at a time of mortal sorrow, send me away,
But welcomed me into his house, and hid his tears;
And all out of pure nobleness and love for me.
Is there a heart more generous in Thessaly
Than his – in all Hellas? Admetus shall not say
His kind act was performed for an ungrateful friend.

Exit HERACLES. *Enter* ADMETUS *and* CHORUS.

ADMETUS: O ravaged house![16] Hateful to come home to,
    Loathsome to look at!
Oh! What grief, shame, remorse, and misery!
I can go nowhere, I can stay nowhere;
Speech is impossible, silence is impossible;
If only I were dead!
For this anguish my mother bore me.
How happy the dead are! Theirs is the peace,
Theirs the dark home I envy and desire.
The sunlight wakes no pleasure in my eyes;
My foot treads the firm earth and feels no joy;
So dear a life was pledged for mine,
Which Death has robbed from me

And delivered to darkness.

CHORUS: Pass on, Admetus; enter your home and hide there.

ADMETUS: I despair.[17]

CHORUS: Despair befits your fate.

ADMETUS: Pity my pain.

CHORUS: Pain overwhelms you, well I know.

ADMETUS: I die for grief.

CHORUS: Your grief cannot help the dead.

ADMETUS: My loss has no end.

CHORUS: Never to see again the face
Of a loving wife – this indeed is loss.

ADMETUS: You touch my heart where the wound lies.
What crueller blow can a man suffer
Than loss of a true wife?
I should never have married,
Never lived with her in this house;
I envy those who are unmarried and childless.
To bear the sorrows of a single life
Is a moderate burden;
But to see children struck by sickness,
A marriage-bed despoiled by death –
This is not tolerable, when one could have chosen
To be unmarried and childless throughout life.

CHORUS: Chance has come upon you; you cannot wrestle
with chance.

ADMETUS: I cannot.

CHORUS: Will you set no bounds to your sorrow?

ADMETUS: No bounds to my sorrow.

CHORUS: Though it is hard to bear, yet none the less –

ADMETUS: Hard to bear.

CHORUS: Endure it. You are not the first that has lost a wife.

ADMETUS: Lost, lost, lost!

CHORUS: In mortal life different events occur
To crush now one man, now another.

ADMETUS: For the beloved lost in the deep earth

Mourning and grief will be long.
Why did you stop me leaping
Into the low grave, to lie
Dead beside the best of women?
So Death would gain, instead of one,
Two faithful souls together
Crossing the lake below the earth.

CHORUS: I had a kinsman lost his only son,
A boy worth weeping for. Nevertheless,
Though childless in old age,
Yet patiently through the grey downward years
He bore his sorrow.

ADMETUS: My handsome house! How can I enter?
How can I live in you, your fortune fallen?
Between that day and this – O bitter change!
Then, with pine-torches from Pelion,
With wedding-songs I was marching in;
I held my loving wife's hand in mine;
A merry company followed with shouts of blessing
On Alcestis, who is dead, and on me.
Two ancient, noble families, they said,
Were joined in one by our marriage.
Now groans cancel that wedding-song;
Gone are my white-clad friends;
Black robes escort me homeward to my desolate bed.

CHORUS: This blow found you unskilled in suffering,
Filled with good fortune.
Your world, your life, are yours today;
But Alcestis has died and left all love behind.
What is strange in this? From many before now
Death has detached their wives.

ADMETUS: Good friends, I count Alcestis' fate more fortunate
Than mine, although it seems not so. For now no pain
Can ever touch her. She has won release from all
Life's troubles with a glorious name; while I have trespassed

Beyond my time. I should not be alive. My life
Will be, as I have learnt too late, a sorry thing.
This house: when I go in, no one to speak to. How
Can I bear it? When I come out, no one speaks to me.
All pleasure's gone. Where shall I turn? The desolation
Indoors will drive me out – her empty bed, the chair
She used to sit in; floors unswept; and round my knees
The children crying for their mother; and the servants
Lamenting the beloved mistress they have lost.
My home will be intolerable. If I go out,
There will be weddings, greetings, gatherings of women –
Alcestis' friends, all young like her: how can I bear
To face them? And behind my back some ill-wisher
Will say, 'There goes the man who did not dare to die,
Who bought a coward's existence at the shameful cost
Of his wife's death; who hates his parents, though he too
Refused to die. Can he pretend to be a man?'
Ill-fame will crown my sorrows. Then, friends, what have I
To live for? My whole life is failure and disgrace.

CHORUS: I have searched through many books,   [Strophe
    I have studied the speculations of astronomers,
    I have pursued innumerable arguments;
    Yet I have found nothing stronger
    Than Necessity. Nor is there any remedy
    Either in the Thracian inscriptions
    Written down from the voice of Orpheus,
    Or in all the salves and simples
    Which Apollo gave to the priests of Asclepius
    To heal the many hurts of mankind.

    Necessity alone has no altar,   [Antistrophe
    No image for men to propitiate,
    Nor does she regard sacrifice.
    May your hand, goddess, in my coming years

Never fall heavier than in the past!
Even Zeus looks for your help
To perform what he ordains.
Steel cannot resist your strength;
In your absolute purpose there is no pity.

You too, Admetus, are held   [Strophe
In Necessity's inescapable bonds.
Harden your heart; never shall your tears
Raise the dead from the depths.
Even the sons of gods
Die and fade into darkness.
Loved while she was with us,
And dead, to be loved for ever,
The noblest of all women
Was she who shared your marriage-bed, Admetus.

Let not Alcestis' monument   [Antistrophe
Be in men's eyes as the graves of mortals.
Let her tomb be honoured like a god's,
Where the passer-by stops to worship;
Turning aside from the road, he will stand and say,
'She, who died for her husband's life,
Is now an immortal being.
Gracious spirit, hear and bless us.'
Such are the prayers that will be said to her.

CHORUS: Look, look, Admetus! If I am not mistaken, here
    Is your guest, Heracles, returning to your house.
Enter HERACLES. *His look is changed; his voice and bearing are*
    those of one relaxed after supreme exertion. A veiled woman follows him.
HERACLES: Admetus, to a friend one should speak openly,
    Not hide reproaches in his heart and say nothing.
    I think you ought to have trusted me to stand by you
    In trouble, and prove myself a friend. You never told me

That your wife's body lay awaiting burial.
You received and feasted me, saying your grief was due
To a stranger's death. I put a garland on my head,
I poured out wine to the gods, while you and all your house
Were in profound distress. You are to blame, my friend,
You are much to blame for treating me in this way. However,
I have no wish to add still further to your grief.

    Listen: I will tell you why I turned back to your house.
I am going now to Thrace, to kill King Diomede
And bring back his wild horses. Will you take this woman
And keep her for me till I return? If I should prove
Unlucky – which may the gods forbid – I give her to you
To serve in your house. It was by a hard struggle
She came into my hands. I found some men arranging
Athletic contests, open to all – well worth a try
For a sportsman; and I won the prize, and here she is.
The prizes given were horses, in the lesser events;
The first prize for the greater, boxing and wrestling, was
A team of oxen, and the girl with them. It seemed wrong
To let slip the good fortune of so fine a prize.
So you must, please, take care of her for me, as I said.
I did not steal her; she is paid for with my own sweat.
Perhaps you too in time to come will give me thanks.

ADMETUS: I did not mean, Heracles, to dishonour you
Or show discourtesy by concealing my wife's death.
But this would have been new pain heaped upon old pain,
To see you stride straight off to stay with another man;
And my own loss already caused me tears enough.
As for this woman, I beg you, if possible, my lord,
Ask someone else, who has not suffered as I have,
To keep her; you have many friends here in this town.
Do not renew my sorrow. Seeing her in the house
Would make me weep – I could not help it. My sick heart
Is heavy enough already; do not add fresh weight
To crush me. In any case, she is young – at least her dress

Suggests it; where then in this house could she be kept?
This is a men's house now, and if she goes about
Among my young men, how can she remain untouched?
It is not easy, Heracles, to rule hot blood –
I speak for your sake. Could she use my dead wife's room,
Sleep in her bed?[18] How can I countenance such a thing?
I fear a double indictment: first, the citizens
Would brand me traitor to the one who saved my life,
Saying I hurried to this girl's embraces; then,
My wife's voice would reproach me – I must reverence her,
I must be very careful what I do. – Young woman,
Whoever you are, you have the same figure and height
Alcestis had; you stand like her. – O gods! Take her,
Take her out of my sight! Why must you ravage me
Twice over? When I look at her, I think I see
My wife. My heart pounds, my eyes flood with tears. I taste
For the first time the full bitterness of despair.

CHORUS: The whims of chance arouse no gratitude in me.
   [To the woman] You must, whoever you are, endure what the
      gods give.

HERACLES: I wish I had such strength as to perform for you
   A friendly service, and bring back to you your wife,
   Up from the house of darkness into this good light.

ADMETUS: I know your goodwill to me; but what help is that?
   It is impossible for the dead to live again.

HERACLES: Bear this with patience; keep your sorrow within
   bounds.

ADMETUS: To give advice is easier than to steel the heart.

HERACLES: If you should weep your whole life through, what
   would you gain?

ADMETUS: Nothing, I know; I am crazed with the desire to
   weep.

HERACLES: The death of one we dearly loved demands our
   tears.

ADMETUS: I die for love of her, even more than I express.

HERACLES: Indeed she was, beyond all denial, a good wife.

ADMETUS: I am one who has no longer any wish to live.

HERACLES: Your wound is fresh now; but with time the pain will ease.

ADMETUS: With time, you say: that time will be the day I die.

HERACLES: A wife will heal you. You will want to marry again.

ADMETUS: Be silent! What a thing to say! I am surprised . . .

HERACLES: At what? Will you not marry? Live a widower?

ADMETUS: No woman living ever shares my bed again.

HERACLES: Do you think that will do Alcestis any good?

ADMETUS: Present or absent, I must always honour her.

HERACLES: Quite right; indeed most right; but you'll be called a fool.

ADMETUS: I swear you'll never call me bridegroom, Heracles.

HERACLES: I'm glad your affection for your wife is so steadfast.

ADMETUS: May heaven strike me dead, if I betray the dead!

HERACLES: And now be generous: take this girl into your house.

ADMETUS: Do not ask that, I entreat, by Zeus who fathered you!

HERACLES: I tell you, it will be an error to refuse.

ADMETUS: If I consent, remorse will gnaw me at the heart.

HERACLES: Consent! Perhaps your kindness will fall fair for you.

ADMETUS: I wish you had never won her in that wrestling-match.

HERACLES: Yet, since I won her, you now share my victory.

ADMETUS: Your words are kind; but let the woman go elsewhere.

HERACLES: She shall go, if she must; but are you sure she must?

ADMETUS: She must — if you will not be angry, Heracles.

HERACLES: There is good reason why I beg so hard for this.

ADMETUS: Win, then; but you are doing something that I hate.

HERACLES: In time, though, you will thank me. Just do as I ask.

ADMETUS [to servants]: It seems we must receive this woman. Take her in.

HERACLES: No; I'll not hand this woman over to your slaves.

ADMETUS: Then, if you wish, lead her into the house yourself.

HERACLES: Oh, no; I insist on giving her into your hands.

ADMETUS: I will not touch her. There's the house; she may go in.

HERACLES: Nothing will satisfy me but your own right hand.

ADMETUS: My lord, I do not wish it. You are forcing me.

HERACLES: Be bold! Stretch out your hand; now take her hand in yours.

ADMETUS [holding out his hand and turning his head away]: There it is! I would as soon cut off the Gorgon's head.

HERACLES joins their hands.

HERACLES: You have her?

ADMETUS: Yes, I have.

HERACLES: Hold her for ever, then;
And tell the son of Zeus he is a generous friend.
Turn round, look at her! Is she something like your wife?
Is she? Now farewell sorrow, welcome happiness!

ADMETUS: O gods! O gods! What marvel is this? Is it true?
I see my wife, her very self! – Or is this joy
Some mockery sent by the gods to drive me mad?

HERACLES: You see no mockery. This is in truth your wife.

ADMETUS: Surely it might be some unreal phantom from the grave?

HERACLES: It was no necromancer that you made your guest.

ADMETUS: I laid her in the grave. Is this my wife I see?

HERACLES: Even so. No wonder you scarcely believe your eyes.

ADMETUS: My wife – alive! May I touch her? May I speak to her?

HERACLES: Yes, speak to her. Your utmost wishes have come true.

ADMETUS: Dearest — your eyes see, and your body lives; it is you!

I thought you lost for ever; and you are mine again.

HERACLES: She is yours indeed. May the gods' envy pass you by!

ADMETUS: Great son of greatest Zeus! May he who fathered you

Prosper and keep you all your days! For you alone

Have raised again my shattered life. All blessing on you!

How did you bring her from that darkness to this light?

HERACLES: I joined battle with Death, who rules the world of spirits.

ADMETUS: This match with Death you speak of — where was it fought out?

HERACLES: I crouched beside the tomb, leaped up, and closed with him.

ADMETUS: Tell me, why does she stand here speaking not a word?

HERACLES: She is still consecrated to the gods below.

Till she is duly purified, and the third dawn

Has risen, it is not lawful for you to hear her voice.

Come, take her in; and, as an honourable man,

Henceforth show perfect piety towards your guests.[19]

Now I will go. Eurystheus king of Argos has

Set me a labour which I must perform. Good-bye!

ADMETUS: Oh, stay with us! Join in our feast and thanks-giving.

HERACLES: Some day, yes. For the present I must lose no time.

ADMETUS: Good luck go with you, and bring you safely here again!

Exit HERACLES.

Pheraeans! I bid you, and our whole land, celebrate

With feasts and dancing this joyful deliverance.
Let every altar flame[20] with pious sacrifice!
The pattern of our life is changed. A better day
Now dawns. I own that Fortune has been kind to me.
CHORUS: Gods manifest themselves in many forms,
Bring many matters to surprising ends.
The things we thought would happen do not happen;
Things unexpected God makes possible;
And that is what has happened here today.

HIPPOLYTUS

CHARACTERS

APHRODITE, *the goddess of sexual love*
HIPPOLYTUS, *bastard son of Theseus*
CHORUS *of huntsmen attending Hippolytus*
SERVANT *of Hippolytus*
CHORUS *of women of Trozen*
NURSE *attending Phaedra*
PHAEDRA, *wife of Theseus*
THESEUS, *king of Athens and Trozen*
MESSENGER
ARTEMIS, *the huntress goddess of virginity*

HIPPOLYTUS

*The scene is before the royal palace at Trozen, where Theseus is
spending a year of voluntary exile to atone for bloodshed. On one
side of the stage is a statue of Aphrodite, on the other a statue of
Artemis. In the centre is the door of the palace.*

Enter APHRODITE.

APHRODITE: Powerful among mortals, glorious among the
    gods,
I am named in earth and heaven the Cyprian,[1] Aphrodite.
From east to west, from the Euxine[2] to the Atlantic Gates,
Over all that see the light of the sun my rule extends.
To those who reverence my power I show favour,
And throw to the earth those I find arrogant and proud.
For gods too have their pride; and it is in their nature
To enjoy receiving honour from the mortal race.

    Hippolytus, the son whom the Amazon[3] bore to Theseus,
Who was trained from childhood by Pittheus the Severe –
This youth, alone among the citizens of Trozen,
Calls me the most pernicious of the heavenly powers.
He abhors the bed of love; marriage he renounces;
Honours instead Apollo's sister, daughter of Zeus,
Artemis – thinks her greatest of all divinities.
All day with her, the virgin, he ranges the green woods,
With his swift hounds emptying the wide earth of beasts,
Too fond of company too high for mortal men.
I do not envy them their sport – I have little cause;
But for his insults, his contempt of me, I shall
Punish Hippolytus this very day. My plans,
Begun already, need but little to perfect.

    Two years ago Hippolytus left Pittheus' house
For Athens, city of Pandion, to witness there

The holy Mysteries and complete his initiation.
And there Phaedra, his father's royal wife, saw him;
And a terrible love,⁴ by my contrivance, gripped her
    heart.
This was before she came with Theseus to Trozen.
There on the very Rock of Pallas, facing west
Toward Trozen, Phaedra built a temple of Aphrodite,
Sick for her absent love; and to this day it bears⁵
Hippolytus' name. Then Theseus, his hands stained with
    blood
Of the Pallantides, to purge his guilt, consented
To live one year in exile, and with his wife set sail
From Athens here to Trozen. So she now, poor wretch,
Groaning and driven mad by the fierce goads of love,
Is dying, and in silence. None of the household knows
What troubles her. But this love shall not end like that.
I will reveal the truth to Theseus; everything
Shall be laid bare; and this young man, my enemy,
His own father shall kill with curses, by the power
Poseidon king of the sea gave him, that three requests
Of Theseus should not fail. Phaedra shall save her honour,
But lose her life; for I will not yield up my rights
Through regard for her misfortunes, but my enemies
Shall pay me their full debt till I am satisfied.

Now I'll retire. Here comes Hippolytus, Theseus' son,
Home after his exertions in the hunting-field,
And at his heels a numerous pack of followers
In full cry, honouring with their songs great Artemis.
He does not know that Death's gates are wide open now,
And that this light he sees today shall be his last.

Exit APHRODITE.

Enter HIPPOLYTUS *with Huntsmen; also an old Servant.*
HIPPOLYTUS: Follow, and sing!
Follow the bright daughter of heaven,
Follow our guardian Maid, Artemis!

HUNTSMEN: Child of Leto and of Zeus,
  Virgin goddess Artemis,
  Great and holy, hear our song.
  Greeting, joyful greeting,
  Loveliest of maidens!
  You who haunt your kingly father's court,
  Tread at ease the broad sky's golden floor,
  Loveliest of immortal maids,
  Joyful greeting, Artemis!

HIPPOLYTUS: Goddess, for you I have twined this crown of
    flowers, gathered
  Fresh from a virgin meadow, where no shepherd dares
  To graze his flock, nor ever yet the scythe swept,
  But bees thread the spring air over the maiden meadow.
  There with clear stream-water Chastity tends the flowers;
  And those whose untaught nature holiness claims entire
  May gather garlands there; and the impure may not.
  Dear mistress, take this circlet for your golden hair,
  Offered with reverent hand. I alone among mortals
  Enjoy this honour, I am your companion, speak with you
  And hear your voice; only your face I do not see.
  And as my life's course has begun, so may it end!

SERVANT: My lord! – or, Prince! for only gods must be
    called lord[6] –
  Would you accept a word of good advice from me?

HIPPOLYTUS: Of course; it would show little wisdom to
    refuse.

SERVANT: You know, then, an old law laid down for mortal
    men –

HIPPOLYTUS: I don't. What law is this you're questioning
    me about?

SERVANT: This law: Abhor pride, and avoid exclusiveness.

HIPPOLYTUS: Quite right; a man who is proud is seldom
    popular.

SERVANT: A man easy to speak with has a certain charm?

HIPPOLYTUS: Great charm indeed, and profit too, with little
    trouble.

SERVANT: Among gods too – do you not expect this law to
    hold?

HIPPOLYTUS: Yes – if we mortals use the same laws as the
    gods.

SERVANT: Then why does a proud goddess get no prayer from
    you?

HIPPOLYTUS: What goddess? Watch your words – they may
    be indiscreet.

SERVANT: She stands here by your palace door: the Cyprian.

HIPPOLYTUS: I greet her from a distance. My body is pure.

SERVANT: Yet she is proud, and mortals greatly honour her.

HIPPOLYTUS: Since gods may choose whom they will honour,
    so may men.

SERVANT: Heaven grant you needful wisdom, and good for-
    tune too!

HIPPOLYTUS: I have no liking for a god worshipped at night.

SERVANT: My son, we should observe the honours due to
    gods.

HIPPOLYTUS: Come, lads, let's go indoors at once; it's time
    for food.
    After hunting, a loaded table's a fine sight.
    And give the horses a rub-down; when I've had my meal
    I'll take them out with the chariot and drive them hard.
    – Your Aphrodite? No! To me she means nothing.
        Exit HIPPOLYTUS *with Huntsmen.*

SERVANT [*turning to the statue of Aphrodite*]: When young men
    show a spirit like his, their ways are not
    For us to copy. In humble words, as fits your servants,
    We pray before your statues, Aphrodite, Queen!
    You must forgive young blood, the eager spirit that utters
    Folly against you. What you heard him say, forget!
    You are a god: gods must be wiser than men are.
        Exit SERVANT. *Enter* CHORUS *of Trozenian Women.*

CHORUS: You know the spot where a rock-face   [Strophe
    Wet with trickling spring-water
    Pours from its top a gushing fountain,
    Where pitchers are dipped in the pool below;
    It was there that a friend of mine,
    Rinsing crimson shawls in the stream
    And spreading them on the sun-baked rock,
    Told me – the first I had heard – about the queen;

    How she languishes on a sick bed,   [Antistrophe
    Keeps always within doors,
    Clouding her golden head in a fine-spun veil.
    They say it is three days now
    That her lips have fasted, that she has kept her body
    Pure[7] from Demeter's grain.
    What suffering wrecks her life she will not tell;
    But she longs to moor in the sad harbour of death.

    Your affliction, Phaedra, is no ecstasy   [Strophe
    Caused by Hecate or Pan; no mountain-wandering
    Such as Cybele sends on the possessed Corybantes.
    Have you offended divine Dictynna?[8]
    Is it neglect of her holy dues
    That wastes you with sickness? Have you failed to offer
    Oil and honey to the Cretan huntress?
    For she roams no less over the salt mere
    And along the sand-bar between eddying waters.[9]

    Or has your noble husband, prince of Erechtheus' [Antistrophe
    sons,
    Found the pastures of pleasure in some secret bed?
    Or has some traveller taken ship from Crete
    To this most hospitable harbour,
    Bringing the queen news of some mischance,
    Whence grief of heart has made her bed her prison?

But there is an unhappy perversity   [Epode
Belonging to women's complex nature –
A despairing helplessness before labour
Causing irrational fancies.
I have felt this wind shudder through my womb;
But I cried aloud to the heavenly helper of women,
Artemis of the arrows;
And always – the gods be praised! – she comes to my deep
   need.

CHORUS: Look! The old Nurse is coming to the door,
Bringing Phaedra into the fresh air.
How weak the queen is, how pale!
I long to know what has so wasted her.
     Enter PHAEDRA *supported by the* NURSE.
     Attendants bring a couch for her.
NURSE: Oh, the sickness and pain of this cruel world!
What would you like me to do, or not to do?
Here you are, in the light, under the clear sky;
We have brought your bed from the palace;
But the cloud on your brow deepens with discontent.
It was here that you begged and longed to come;
Soon you'll be fretting for your room again.
Each minute cheats you, nothing gives you pleasure;
You hate what you have, and crave what you have not.
Better to be sick, which is a single trouble,
Than wait on the sick, which troubles both heart and hand.
The whole of our life is full of pain,
And sorrow finds no relief.
And after this life, is there a happier world?[10]
That is concealed from us, wrapped in clouds and darkness.
The truth stands plain: that we blindly love,
Such as it is, our little gleam of day.
For we know nothing of any other life;
The world below is a mystery;

And we are carried along with foolish tales.
Servants have now placed PHAEDRA *on her couch.*
PHAEDRA: Support my body. Hold my head up.
The strength of my limbs has melted away.
Girls, hold my hands, my shapely arms.
This cap is heavy on my head – take it off;
Now let my hair fall round my shoulders.
NURSE: Patience, child!
Don't tire yourself with tossing to and fro.
If you are quiet and keep a brave heart
Your illness will be easier to bear.
We are mortal, and so must suffer.
PHAEDRA: Oh! Oh! To kneel by a fountain in the fresh dew
And drink a cupful of clear water!
To lie under the poplar trees
And rest deep in the waving grass!
NURSE: What are you saying, child? Don't scatter words
So recklessly – there are people here!
Such speech is mounted on madness.
PHAEDRA: Come, all of you, take me out to the hills!
I'm going to the woods, through the pine-forests
Where hounds pace after blood
And press close on the spotted deer.
For the gods' sake, take me! How I long to be there,
Shouting to the pack,
Lifting a lance to my hair bright in the wind,
Gripping a barbed spear!
NURSE: What is it, child, you are fretting for?
What are hounds and the hunt to you?
If you are thirsty,
Here by the palace wall a stream runs down the hill.
PHAEDRA: Artemis of the salt mere,
Goddess of the race-course and rattling hooves,
O for your level rides,
And the tamed strength of Thessaly horses under my hand!

NURSE: Again these wild words! Are you out of your mind?
   A moment past you were off to the hills,
   Hunting as you wanted to;
   Now you long for a horse on a dry sandy track.
   Here's a task for a prophet indeed, to guess
   Which of the gods has his bridle on you
   And drives you beside yourself, my daughter!

PHAEDRA: Oh, gods have pity! Whatever did I do?
   How far did I stray from sanity?
   I was mad; a malign god struck me down.
   What shall I do? What will become of me?
   Dear Nurse, my veil again;
   I am ashamed to think what I have said.
   Cover me; my tears are falling,
   And my face is hot with shame.
   To be in my right mind is agony;
   Yet to be mad was intolerable.
   It is best, then, to be aware of nothing,
   And die.

NURSE [veiling her]: There, child, there! – How soon
   Shall my face too be veiled with death?
   I have lived long, and learnt much.
   Since everyone must die, it would be better
   That friends should set a limit to affection,
   And never open their hearts' depths to each other.
   The ties of love ought to lie loosely on us,
   Easy to slip or tighten.
   For one heart to endure the pain of two,
   As I suffer for her, is a cruel burden.
   They say that exact and scrupulous conduct
   Brings with it more trouble than pleasure
   And is an enemy to health.
   So I'm tired of selfless devotion;
   I think the best rule is, *A limit to everything*;
   And any wise man will say the same.

CHORUS: Nurse, the queen's pitiful distress is clear to us;
   But what her illness is we cannot understand.

   May we not hear from you, her old and trusted servant?
NURSE: I have questioned her. She will not speak. I know
    nothing.
CHORUS: Not even how, or when, this trouble first began?
NURSE: The same answer: to all such questions, not a word.
CHORUS: Her body seems so wasted; all her strength is gone.
NURSE: No wonder; she has eaten nothing for three days.
CHORUS: Is this a god-sent folly, or a plain wish to die?
NURSE: How should I know? But die she will, if she won't eat.
CHORUS: Surely her husband's not content to let her die?
NURSE: She hides her illness, tells her husband she is well.
CHORUS: Can he not see the truth by looking in her face?
NURSE: No; as it happens, Theseus is away from Trozen.
CHORUS: This sickness, these delusions, follow from some
    cause:
   Have you no way to make her tell you what it is?
NURSE: I have tried every thing, and met with no success;
   But even now I'll do my best, and not give up.
   And you, ladies, can bear me witness, since you're here,
   That I stand by her faithfully in time of need.

    Dear child, let's both forget the things we said before.
   And you, be kinder — smooth out this resentful brow,
   Unknot your thoughts; and I, where I misunderstood
   Before, will start afresh and take a wiser course.
   Is your affliction one you cannot openly
   Speak of? These women here can help with remedies.
   But if your trouble can be told to a man, then speak,
   And we will consult doctors. Well? Still not a word?
   My dear, if I have spoken foolishly, correct me;
   If well, say you agree; but do not sit there dumb!
   Say something! Look at me! — Oh, friends, it is no use;
   It's wasted labour. She would not relent before,
   And still won't listen. We're as far off as we were.

— Look here, then: you may prove more stubborn than the
   sea;
But if you die — mark me, you have betrayed your sons.
They'll never be inheritors of their father's house —
No, by Hippolyta, queen of the riding Amazons!
She bore a son whom your two boys will serve as slaves,
A bastard full of royal ambition — you know him well:
Hippolytus!

PHAEDRA: No! Oh, no!

NURSE: Ha! Does that touch you?

PHAEDRA: Nurse,
   You kill me! I implore you, in the name of the gods,
   Never again to speak of him.

NURSE: There, now! You're not
   Out of your mind — far from it. Yet you still refuse
   Either to help your children or to save your life.

PHAEDRA: I love them both. A different storm is wrecking
   me.

NURSE: My daughter, are your hands pure from any guilt of
   blood?

PHAEDRA: My hands are pure. It is my heart that is defiled.

NURSE: What? By a wrong some enemy has done to you?

PHAEDRA: A friend[11] kills me; and no more by his will than
   mine.

NURSE: Is Theseus guilty? Has he done you some injury?

PHAEDRA: No, no! May I be found as guiltless towards him!

NURSE: What is this terror, then, which makes you long to
   die?

PHAEDRA: Leave me to sin alone. I do not injure *you*.

NURSE: Willingly, never! If I fail, the fault's not mine.

PHAEDRA: You'd force me? You forget yourself — let my hand
   go!

NURSE: Your hand, your knees too — no, I'll never let you go!

PHAEDRA: Poor soul! For you, too, knowing would be
   terrible.

NURSE: For me, what could be worse than not to win your trust?

PHAEDRA: It would kill you. Yet what I am doing is for my honour.

NURSE: If so, I am right to implore you – speak! Why hide the truth?

PHAEDRA: I am contriving to bring honour out of shame.

NURSE: To speak, then, will enhance your honour before the world.

PHAEDRA: Go away now, for the gods' sake, and let go my hand.

NURSE: I won't; this is a gift you owe, and still refuse.

PHAEDRA: I'll give it, then. I can't refuse your suppliant hand.

NURSE: I will be quiet. Now it is for you to speak.

PHAEDRA: My mother![12] Oh, what pitiful passion raged in you!

NURSE: My child, what's this? You mean her craving for the bull?

PHAEDRA: Your anguish too, my sister, whom Dionysus loved!

NURSE: Why raise these evil memories of your family?

PHAEDRA: I am the third. The curse that struck them now kills me.

NURSE: You frighten me. What horror will you come to next?

PHAEDRA: My wretched fate began with them; it is not new.

NURSE: You still tell me no more of what I want to hear.

PHAEDRA: If only you could say for me what I must say!

NURSE: Well, I'm no soothsayer, to read your hidden thoughts.

PHAEDRA: When people say they are in love, what do they mean?

NURSE: Dear child! A very sweet thing, and yet full of pain.

PHAEDRA: I seem to have missed the sweetness and embraced the pain.

NURSE: What are you saying, my daughter? You love a man?
    What man?

PHAEDRA: Why, who else should it be? It is he, the
    Amazon's –

NURSE: You mean Hippolytus?

PHAEDRA: You spoke his name, not I.

NURSE: Oh, child, what will you say? Oh, you have broken
    my heart!

  Oh, friends, how can I bear it? I don't want to live!
  Oh, hateful day! This hateful life!

She collapses to the ground, and the CHORUS *come to help her*
                                              No, let me fall,
  Leave me alone, I want to die and be at peace.
  I am dying, my life is over! . . . What does it mean?
  A good, pure-hearted woman lusting after sin
  Against her own will! Aphrodite is no god!
  She is something different, something greater – she it is
  Who has brought the queen, and me, and this whole house
    to ruin.

CHORUS: Did you hear? Oh, did you hear?
  The queen's pitiful words
  That tell of a fate too cruel for hearing?
  Beloved queen, let me die
  Before my heart should know your heart's despair!
  Oh, Phaedra, daughter of sorrow!
  Oh, sorrow, nurse of our race!
  Oh, deadly truth brought into sudden light!
  What now awaits you every hour of this day?
  Fate hangs unknown over your house.
  Aphrodite sent you an unhappy star,
  Princess of Crete;
  We see now where it will sink and set.

        PHAEDRA *has left her bed and moved downstage.*

PHAEDRA: Women of Trozen, who live here on the eastern
    edge

Of Peloponnese: I have at times lain long awake
In the night, thinking of human lives that have collapsed
In ruin. Deterioration, I believe, does not
Arise from inborn folly; since, of those who fail,
Many are virtuous; but it seems more true to say
That, though knowledge and judgement tell us what is good,
We don't act out our knowledge — some through indolence,
Others through valuing some other pleasure more
Than goodness; and our life offers us many pleasures.[13]
    Since, then, this is in fact my view, there is no spell
That could induce me to be false to it, or fall
Into a pose which contradicts my own judgement.
So I must trace for you the path my thoughts followed.
When love struck me, I searched for the best way to endure
The wound. My first resolve was to let slip no word,
Hide what I suffered. For there's no trusting the tongue,
Which knows how to instruct other men's purposes,
But by its folly draws disaster on itself.
Next, I prepared to endure this madness as I ought
By mastering it with self-control. But finally,
When I could not subdue the goddess by these means,
I knew — and beyond contradiction — that for me
The best of all decisions was to end my life.
I would not wish my right action to rest unknown,
Any more than to display my sin before the world.
What I desired, and the desire itself, I knew,
Were both dishonourable. I knew too, and too well,
I was a woman — a thing hated by everyone.
Whatever woman first betrayed her marriage-bed
With other men, all deadly curses crowd on her!
It was from noble houses that this plague first fell
On women; when the high-born choose a shameful course,
The common herd will surely find it right for them.
I hate those women whose tongues talk of chastity,
Who all the while are bold in every secret sin.

Oh, sovereign, sea-born Aphrodite! How can they
Look in their husbands' eyes, without a shudder felt
Lest sheltering darkness and their guilty walls should speak?
   It is for this, friends, that I am dying; I will never
Be known to bring dishonour on my husband or
My children. I want my two sons to go back and live
In glorious Athens, hold their heads high there, and speak
Their mind like free men, honoured for their mother's
   name.
One thing can make the most bold-spirited man a slave:
To know the secret of a parent's shameful act.
They say that a clear conscience and an upright heart
Alone gives strength to wrestle in the trials of life;
While evil-doers, soon or late — as a young girl
Sees truth in a glass — so they, when Time holds up his
   mirror,
Are exposed. May I never be seen as one of them!
CHORUS: It is true: wherever virtue lives, her face is noble;
   And the fruit of virtue in this life is a good name.
NURSE: My lady, when I heard, a moment since, of your
   Trouble, at the first shock I was terrified; but now
   It strikes me I was foolish. Often in human life
   Our second thoughts are wiser. What has happened to you
   Is nothing extraordinary or hard to understand.
   The strong fever of Aphrodite has struck at you:
   You're in love. Is that surprising? So are many others.
   Are you to lose your life, then, because love has come?
   There's surely a grim prospect for all lovers now
   And in the future, if their duty is to die!
   When Love sweeps on you in her full power, to resist
   Is perilous. She steals gently on those who yield to her;
   But someone she finds full of pride and arrogance —
   Why, what do you think? — she takes and tramples in the
      dust!
   Love wanders the high heavens; in the swollen sea

You'll find her; the whole universe was born from Love.
She sows all seeds; and that eager desire from which
Each earthly generation springs — this is her gift.
Those who have pictures painted in times past, or spend
Their days in reading, know that Zeus once fell in love
With Semele; they know that Cephalus was once
Snatched up to heaven by the glorious glowing Dawn
Because she loved him. Now they both live in the sky,
And show no haste to quit the company of gods.
Events defeat them; and they are, I think, content.
     And *you* won't yield? Your father should have begotten
     you
On stated terms, or under the rule of different gods,
If you decline to accept these elementary laws.
How many good and sensible husbands, do you suppose,
Seeing their wives unfaithful, look the other way?
How many fathers help their reckless, love-sick sons
To gain their object? Look: to keep faults out of sight
Is mortal wisdom. It's not for us to struggle after
Tiresome perfection. Does a builder plane and polish
The rafters in the roof? No. And, in any case,
How are you going to swim clear of this flood of trouble
You've met with? You are mortal, and if your life holds
More good than bad, you can be called most fortunate.
     My daughter, soften your stubborn heart; do not blas-
     pheme.
Well, what is it but blasphemy, to wish yourself
Stronger than a god? Be bold, and love; this is god's will.
Since you are stricken, turn the stroke to your own good.
Why, there are spells; and words can act as soothing charms.
Trouble may wait a precious time for men to mend it —
Unless a woman gets to work and finds the way.
CHORUS: For present need, her counsel is more practical,
     Phaedra; though you, I think, are right. But it may be
     That my approval is harder for you to accept

Than her rebukes, and more disagreeable to hear.

PHAEDRA: This is what brings destruction on our fine cities
    And ancient families — fair speech, too fair by far!
    Instead of saying what you think will flatter me,
    Give me sound counsel which will keep my honour safe.

NURSE: Such high-flown talk! It's not fine sentiments you
        need;
    You must have your man. Someone must tell him in plain
        terms
    What's happened, and persuade him without more delay.
    If this were not a matter of life and death, if you
    Were still a chaste wife, I would never encourage you
    So far for lust and pleasure; but our work's cut out
    To save your life — there's nothing odious in that.

PHAEDRA: It appals me to hear you. Nothing odious?
    Be silent, never speak such shameful words again.

NURSE: Yes, shameful; but more use to you than virtuous
        words.
    Better to do the thing you want to do, and save
    Your life, than die for the vain boast of chastity.

PHAEDRA: I beg you! What you say is plausible, but vile.
    Not one more word! My heart is like a field long tilled
    By love; if you're so eloquent for evil, I
    Shall be launched helpless toward that end I fly from now.

NURSE: Have it your own way. You ought not to be in
        love;
    But since you are, do as I say — which is next best.
    I have indoors a medicine which can soothe your love —
    I've only now remembered. It will cause you no
    Disgrace, nor harm your wits; but it will put an end —
    If you are not faint-hearted — to your malady.
    We need to get some token from the man desired —
    A lock of hair, some scrap of clothing; and then join
    Token and spell to bring about a happy issue.

PHAEDRA: This drug you have — is it an ointment or a draught?

NURSE: I don't know. Look for satisfaction, girl; why ask
    Questions?
PHAEDRA: I dread it. You may prove to be too clever.
NURSE: You'd be afraid of anything. What do you dread?
PHAEDRA: That you speak any word of me to Theseus' son.
NURSE: Leave all to me, child; I know how to manage this.
    [*Aside*] Only stand by me, great Queen Aphrodite, now,
    And be my accomplice! – For what else I have in mind,
    A word with friends inside the palace will be enough.
              Exit NURSE. PHAEDRA *remains.*
CHORUS: Eros, you who distil   [*Strophe*
    The dew of longing upon lovers' eyes,
    Eros, you who invade
    With gentle joy those hearts you mark for conquest;
    Rise not in cruelty, I pray,
    Come not in violence!
    Neither fire-blast nor star-stroke is more fearful
    Than Aphrodite's dart which flies
    From the hand of Eros, child of Zeus.

    In vain by Alpheus' banks,   [*Antistrophe*
    In vain shall Hellas at Apollo's Pythian shrine
    Multiply the slaughter of bulls,
    While Eros, monarch of men, who holds
    Aphrodite's key to her chamber of dear delight –
    Him we neglect to worship;
    Love, whose coming is devastation
    And every mortal calamity.

    Iole, princess of Oechalia,   [*Strophe*
    Was once a virgin, knew neither man nor marriage,
    A filly still unyoked;
    And Aphrodite took her from her father's home,
    A wild nymph, helpless and frantic;
    And there, as death raged and smoke arose,

Gave her in blood-sealed union to Alcmene's son.
O Iole, what misery was your marriage!

O holy wall of Thebes,   [*Antistrophe*
O lips of the Dircean spring,
You with one voice could tell
How terrible is the advent of Aphrodite.
When thunder and flame fell upon Semele
And she gave birth to Bacchus, son of Zeus,
Aphrodite laid her to bed,
A bride in the embrace of Death.
The breath of her terror is felt in every land,
And as a bee's flight is the path of her power.

> *During the last stanza* PHAEDRA *has moved to the
> door of the palace, and stands listening.*

PHAEDRA: Be silent, women. Oh, the last blow has fallen
   now.
CHORUS: What terrible thing, Phaedra, is happening in the
   house?
PHAEDRA: Wait, now; I want to hear exactly what they say.
CHORUS: I will be quiet. From what you say I fear the worst.
PHAEDRA: Oh, no, no, no, no!
   Why must I suffer so? It is unbearable!
CHORUS: What is unbearable? What is this anguished cry?
   Tell us, what word
   Fell on your heart like a storm of terror?
PHAEDRA: A word that kills me. Come and stand here near
   the door
   And listen to the uproar filling the whole house.
CHORUS: You are beside the door;[14]
   News from the house is for you to tell.
   Speak, then; tell us what dreadful thing has happened.
PHAEDRA: That shouting – it is the son of the riding Amazon,
   Hippolytus,[15] reviling, execrating my servant.
CHORUS: I hear the sound, but nothing clearly.

You heard that cry from the house –
Tell us what was said.

PHAEDRA: It is clear enough; he is calling her a 'filthy bawd',
Abusing her as 'traitress to her master's bed'.

CHORUS: What a terrible thing – dear Phaedra, you are
betrayed.
What can I do to help?
Your secret shown to the world – what misery! –
Your life destroyed by a friend you trusted.

PHAEDRA: She has told him the whole fatal truth. She spoke
in love,
Meaning to heal my suffering. But it was a crime!

CHORUS: What then? Do you see any way out? What will you
do?

PHAEDRA: I know only one thing, that death must end this
torture
As soon as possible. There's no other remedy.

Enter HIPPOLYTUS *followed by the* NURSE.

HIPPOLYTUS: O mother earth! Unfolded radiance of the sun!
What sickening speech, what outrage I have listened to!

NURSE: Dear lad, be quiet, stop shouting, before someone
hears.

HIPPOLYTUS: What I have heard is criminal. How can I keep
quiet?

NURSE: Do stop! I kneel, I beg you by your strong right hand.

HIPPOLYTUS: How dare you touch me? Away! Keep your
hands off my clothes.

NURSE: Don't tell what I said, don't destroy me altogether.

HIPPOLYTUS: Destroy? How's that? You tell me you said
nothing wrong.

NURSE: What I said, son, was not for everyone to hear.

HIPPOLYTUS: Should honest words be hushed up? Let everyone hear!

NURSE: Dear boy, you'll never slight the oath you swore to
me?

HIPPOLYTUS: It was my tongue that swore it. No oath binds
   my heart.

NURSE: What will you do? Destroy someone so near to you?

HIPPOLYTUS: I spit your word out. Criminals have no claim
   on me.

NURSE: Forgive, son; we are human, we do wrong by nature.

HIPPOLYTUS: O Zeus! Why have you established in the
   sunlit world

This counterfeit coin, woman, to curse the human race?
If you desired to plant a mortal stock, why must
The means for this be women? A better plan would be
For men to come to your temples and put down a price
In bronze, or iron, or weight of gold, and buy their sons
In embryo, for a sum befitting each man's wealth.
Then they could live at home like free men – without
   women.

Look – here's your proof that woman is an evil pest:
Her father, who begot her and brought her up, then adds
A dowry for her; this gets her a home, and he
Gets rid of his load. The man who takes this noxious weed
Into his home now rapturously decks his idol
With gauds and gowns, heaps beauty on hatefulness, poor
   wretch,
Squandering the family fortune. For an easy life
At home, to marry a cipher might be best – except
That no good comes of inanity on a pedestal.
Yet a clever woman, with more wit than becomes a woman,
I abhor; I would not have such a woman in my house.
The sexual urge breeds wickedness more readily
In clever women; while the incompetent are saved
From wantonness by lack of wit. A woman should have
No servant ever come near her; she should live attended
By dumb and savage beasts; then she could neither speak
To anyone, nor have any servant reply to her.
As it is, unchaste wives brood on unchastity

At home, while servants traffic their lewdness to the world –
Yes, you, for one, who come here like a she-devil
Inviting me to incest with my father's wife!
I'll flush my ears with water to purge your filthy words!
Do you think I could so sin, when even hearing you
I feel polluted? One thing saves you, woman: I fear
The gods. You trapped me, and I rashly gave my oath;
Otherwise I'd have told my father the whole story.
Instead, I shall now leave this house till he comes back;
And I'll say nothing; but I shall come back with him,
And observe how you – yes, and your mistress – meet his eye.

My curse on the whole race of women! I shall never
Be sated with my loathing of you. People tell me
I always say this. Why not? Women, it seems, are always
Evil. So, whoever can teach them to be chaste
May forbid me to tread them down with infamy.

Exit HIPPOLYTUS.

PHAEDRA: How cruel a curse it is to be born a woman!
Who would not pity us?
What shift, what resource have we,
What words, once we have stumbled,
To undo the knot a word has tied?
I have met what I deserved. Earth and sunlight,
Where shall I fly out of the clutch of Fate?
How can I hide this agony?
What god could appear to help me,
What mortal man would stand
As my counsellor or partner in wickedness?
My passion reaches the boundary of life,
And the passing is cruel.
Is there another woman so abused by Chance?

CHORUS: I weep for you. The harm is done; your servant's
plans
Have all miscarried, lady, and evil is afoot.

PHAEDRA: You vicious, vile betrayer of your friends, see now

What you've done to me! Zeus, who gave me life, blast you
With fire, destroy you root and branch! Did I not say —
Did I not guess what you intended, and forbid
You speak one word of what now drags me in the dirt?
Now your incontinence will rob even my death
Of honour. Well, some new plan now must be thought out.
Hippolytus, white-hot with rage, will denounce *me*
To his father for *your* wickedness, fill the whole land
With his outrageous narrative! My curse on you!
My curse on all officious fools who wickedly
Thrust their unwanted help on friends to ruin them!

NURSE: Mistress, you may indeed blame me for doing wrong;
   Your wound is smarting, and your judgement's overborne;
   But, if you'll hear me, I can speak in my defence.
   I brought you up; I am your friend. I tried to find
   A remedy for your sickness — but the one I found
   Was not what I had hoped to find. If I'd succeeded,
   Everyone would have reckoned me a wise woman.
   They call it wisdom when we happen to guess right.

PHAEDRA: Indeed! You think this fair, this good enough for
   me —
   Wound me to death, then word me in this magnanimous
   tone!

NURSE: We're talking too much. I admit I was unwise.
   Yet, dear child, bad as things are, still there's life, there's
   hope!

PHAEDRA: Stop! No more words! You gave me bad advice
   before,
   And wicked help. Out of my sight! Scheme for your own
   Affairs; and I will order mine as they should be.

Exit NURSE.

   Do me this favour, noblewomen of Trozen:
   Bury in silence all that you have heard today.

CHORUS: I swear by Zeus's daughter, holy Artemis,
   To disclose nothing of what you have suffered here.

PHAEDRA: Thanks for that promise. One thing further I will
      tell.
   I have found a way – a way, indeed – to cure this ill,
   To ensure an honourable future for my two sons,
   And gain for me what can be saved from today's wreck.[16]
   The royal house of Crete shall suffer no disgrace
   By me; nor will I, to preserve a single life,
   Meet Theseus face to face knowing dishonour done.
CHORUS: What is this deed past remedy that you intend?
PHAEDRA: To die; but how I'll order it, is mine to choose.
CHORUS: Keep your lips pure!
PHAEDRA: You likewise, give me pure advice.
   Today I shall be rid of life, and so shall give
   Pleasure to Aphrodite, who is my destroyer;
   And I shall die defeated; love is merciless.
   Yet my death shall prove fatal to another's life
   And teach him to ride roughshod on my misery.
   He shall share equally in my sickness, and learn
   That chastity is humility and gentleness.[17]

               PHAEDRA *goes into the palace.*

CHORUS: O to escape, and lurk high under   [*Strophe*
      steep crags,
   At the touch of a god to rise,
   A wing'd bird among flying flocks!
   To soar over the swell of the Adrian coast,
   Above the waters of Eridanos
   Where, in lament for Phaethon,
   His sisters drop their piteous tears
   Which glow like amber in the dark stream;

   And then to reach that shore planted with   [*Antistrophe*
      apple-trees
   Where the daughters of evening sing,
   Where the sea-lord of the dark shallows
   Permits to sailors no further passage,

Establishing the solemn frontier of heaven
Which Atlas guards;
Where divine fountains flow beside Zeus's marriage-bed;
Where holy earth offers her choice fruits
To enrich the blissful gods.

O white-wing'd Cretan ship   [*Strophe*
Which carried my lady Phaedra from her royal home
Over the salt swell of the pounding sea —
The happy bride you brought was set for sorrow;
The hour was ominous both when she flew forth
From the land of Minos to glorious Athens,
And again when on the rocky shore of Mounichos
They made fast their twisted hawser-ends
And stepped on to mainland soil.

So it was that, with a fearful sickness of   [*Antistrophe*
     unholy passion,
Aphrodite shattered her heart.
Now, foundering under cruel mischance,
She will fasten a hanging noose
To the beams of her bridal chamber,
Fitting it around her pale throat;
Crushed with shame at her hateful destiny,
She will choose instead the glory of good repute,
And rid her heart of its anguished longing.
     A voice is heard from inside the palace.
VOICE: Oh, help, help! Anyone in the palace, come and help!
     Our mistress — she is hanging, strangling — Theseus' wife!
CHORUS: It is done, then, and all over now. The queen is
     dead.
     She tied a noose, fastened the rope, and hanged herself!
VOICE: Where are you all? Come quickly, bring a knife, a
     sword —
     Something to cut this cord knotted around her neck.

CHORUS: – What shall we do, friends? Do you think we
 should go inside
 And try to set the queen free from the tightened noose?
 – Why should we? Has she not young men attending her?
 To interfere like that is always dangerous.

VOICE: She's dead, poor lady! Lay her straight, compose her
 limbs.
 Oh, what a bitter tale to have to tell my master!

CHORUS: Did you hear that? Poor Phaedra, then, has breathed
 her last;
 They are already laying out her lifeless body.

Enter THESEUS, *attended. His head is crowned with the garland
worn by those who have received a favourable answer from an oracle.*

THESEUS: Do you know, women, what was that distressful cry
 Inside the palace, which reached my ears a moment since?
 This is strange; when I come home from a pious mission,
 My house receives me with shut doors, and not a word
 Of loyal welcome! There is no bad news, I trust,
 Of Pittheus? He is well advanced in years; but still
 His departure from this house would be a grief to me.

CHORUS: No, Theseus. What has happened to you does not
 concern
 The old. It is the young whose death must break your heart.

THESEUS: Oh, no! Don't say my children's lives are robbed
 from me!

CHORUS: They live. The worst of all is true: their mother is
 dead.

THESEUS: My wife – what do you say? She's dead? What happened, then?

CHORUS: She took a cord and made a noose and hanged
 herself.

THESEUS: But what occurred to cause this? Was she numbed
 with grief?

CHORUS: That is all I know, Theseus. I too have just arrived
 At the palace, as a mourner for your grievous loss.

THESEUS: Why have I wreathed this leafy garland round my
head?
Here is my cruel answer from the oracle!
Ho, there! Servants! Unbar these doors and open wide!
Open them, let me see a sight to blast my eyes –
See my dead wife, whose death is living death to me!

The doors open, showing PHAEDRA *dead.*

CHORUS: Weep for the queen, tears for her tears.
Phaedra, your agony and your act alike
Must banish peace from this house.
How could you dare a death so hideous, so unholy,
A prey to your own pitiless hand?
And who, poor soul, has dimmed and quenched your life?

THESEUS: O the misery of the world! Here I have suffered
The heaviest of all my sorrows. O Chance,
How cruelly you have assaulted me and my house –
Sent as a nameless taint from some malign power;
Worse, an annihilation of life and the love of life!
I strain despairing eyes over my sea of misery;
Hope vanishes, the shore is out of sight;
Disaster is a wave that I cannot surmount.
What piteous word can I speak, dear wife,
What fated cruelty can I accuse?
As a bird from my hand you have vanished,
Swooped swift and daring into the pit of darkness,
And left me tears for your death and anguish for your
despair.[18]
From some distant age,
From sin committed in time long past,
I reap this harvest which the gods have sent.

CHORUS: This sorrow, king, has fallen not on you alone;
A good wife's loss is one that many others share.

THESEUS: Below the earth, the gloom below the earth –
Now let me die, and go,
And make my joyless home there,

Since you, dearer than all, are at my side no more,
And the death you dealt surpasses the death that took you.
What was it? Whence, my wife, could it come –
This chance whose deadly blow tortured your heart?
Will someone tell me what happened here? Or does my
    palace
Harbour a useless rabble of king's lackeys?
Oh, Phaedra, my heart is broken. Friends, pity me,
Who have lived to see such pain ravage my home;
A pain no heart could bear, no words describe.
Oh, my life is ended, my house desolate,
My children motherless. Dear Phaedra,
You left us, you left us – you, the best
Of all women that the dazzling sun beholds,
Or the starry face of night.

> *As* THESEUS *has been speaking, the* CHORUS *has
> noticed a letter tied to* PHAEDRA'S *wrist.*

CHORUS: I pity you, Theseus,
For the evil your house is involved in.
Yet, while I watch your sorrow with tear-filled eyes,
I tremble with deeper dread for the terror to come.

THESEUS: But look! Look here! What's this, fastened to her
    dear hand?
A letter! With a message for me – something new?
Did she write telling me her last sad thoughts about
Our love, our children, bidding me remember them?
Rest easy, Phaedra! Theseus' house and bed shall never
Be entered by another woman. – See, the imprint
Here of her golden signet brings me from the dead
Her greeting, her caress! Now to untwist the thread
From the seal – what will this letter have to say to me?

CHORUS: Here is a new terror
Sent by the gods to crown the rest.
After the act already accomplished
What further blow could fall now?

Pity our king, pity him –
His house heaped in ruin, never to rise!

THESEUS: Oh, oh! Horror upon horror! How can I speak
it?

CHORUS: What is it, Theseus? Tell us, if it is for us to hear.

THESEUS: The letter – it shrieks, it howls horrors insuffer-
able!
I am crushed; where can I escape?
What I have seen has killed me.
A voice from the letter speaks
And tells – what things! what things!

CHORUS: What terrible disclosure can your words forebode?

THESEUS: A wickedness so dreadful
That I can scarcely force my tongue to speak it;
Yet I will not hold back. Listen, O city:
Hippolytus has dared to affront the holy eye
Of great Zeus, and with violence to enter my bed.
Then, my father Poseidon, since you promised me
Three curses, with one of them now strike down my son!
If they were valid curses that you gave me then,
Let my son not escape his fate to this day's end!

CHORUS: In the gods' name, my lord, take back the curse you
have uttered.
Believe me, you are mistaken – as you will learn in time.

THESEUS: Impossible! And I add to my curse banishment:
If he escape one fate he shall fall by the other.
Either Poseidon will respect the curse I spoke
And send him dead to the dark realm below the earth,
Or else he shall, a wandering outcast from this country,
On foreign soil drain to the dregs his wretched life.

CHORUS: Why, here this very moment comes your son him-
self,
Hippolytus. King Theseus, calm this perilous rage,
And think what action will best serve your family.

Enter HIPPOLYTUS *with other young noblemen.*[19]

HIPPOLYTUS: I heard your cry, father, and I have come at
    once;
    But what the matter is which causes you this grief
    I do not know — so I would wish to learn from you.
    — Oh! What do I see here? Father, it is your wife —
    Dead! I am utterly astonished! It was only
    Just now that I was leaving her. She was alive
    A short time since. What happened to her? How did she die?
    Father! I wish to learn what happened, and from you.
    You are silent? Silence is out of place at such a moment.
    It is not right — since I am a friend, and something more
    Than a friend, father — to hide your suffering from me.
THESEUS: O futile humans! Why, why does your manifold
    folly
    Teach skills innumerable, devise, discover all
    Other use; but there's one knowledge you do not gain,
    One quarry you have not hunted down, and that's the skill
    To implant a right mind in a brutish, coarse nature.
HIPPOLYTUS: He certainly would be a clever instructor who
    Could drive sense into a fool. But, father, this is not
    The right moment for philosophical subtlety.
    Excess of sorrow, I fear, has made your tongue run wild.
THESEUS: There should be somewhere a touchstone of human
    hearts
    Which men could trust to sift the thoughts of friends, and
    show
    Which one is a true friend and which is treacherous.
    Each man should have two voices: the one an honest voice,
    The other — natural; so that his lying voice might be
    Refuted by the true; and we should not be duped.
HIPPOLYTUS: Why, has some whispering friend contrived to
    slander me?
    Have I now fallen suspect, guiltless as I am?
    This is amazing! Yes — that *you* should speak such words
    Amazes me. Clearly your wits have gone astray.

THESEUS: The heart of man! Is there no crime it will not dare?
　　Can no limit be set to brazen wickedness?
　　If in one lifetime it will swell and bulk so huge,
　　If each new age deploys worse villainy than the last,
　　The gods will need to create a second earth, to house
　　Such vicious, corrupt natures as this world rejects.
　　Look at this man, who, being my son, has shamed my bed;
　　Who is proved guilty by the damning testimony
　　Of her dead hand! – Come, show your face, since I'm already
　　Polluted by your presence; look me in the eyes –
　　Your father! So, you are the man above other men,
　　One who consorts with gods, whose life is chaste, un-
　　　smirched
　　With evil! Who believes your boasts? Who is the fool
　　Who charges gods with ignorance? Not I! So now
　　Take Orpheus for your master, dance his crazy rites
　　And reverently recite his wordy vapourings!
　　Yes, you've been caught. Let all take warning: of such men
　　Beware! With lofty phrases they pursue their prey
　　To shameful purpose. – Oh, she is dead, you'll say. Does that
　　Seem to acquit you? It is prime proof of your guilt,
　　Vile wretch! What oaths, what arguments could outweigh
　　　this
　　Dead body, and clear you from this charge? Or will you say
　　She hated you – that enmity is natural
　　Between the bastard and the freeborn? Was she then
　　So poor a bargainer with her life, to throw away
　　Its youth and sweetness out of spite to you? Perhaps
　　You'll tell me men are wanting in lasciviousness,
　　Women more prone to it? Take my word – a young man's
　　　not
　　Any steadier than a woman, when his youthful heart
　　Is set aflame by Aphrodite; but his sex
　　Itself gives him advantage. So then – and yet why
　　Should I thus fight down your defence, when her dead body

Blazons its evidence to my eyes? Out of this land
To exile! Go, I say! Never again approach
The god-built city of Athens, cross no boundary
That my sword guards. I tell you, if I weaken before
This outrage, Sinis the Isthmian bandit will take oath
I never killed him, call me boaster; and those rocks[20]
Washed by the sea, where Sciron perished, shall forget
The deadly weight of my hand against evildoers.

CHORUS: Can any mortal man be named as fortunate?
     None; the most firm prosperity is overturned.

HIPPOLYTUS: Father, your vehemence and intensity of
     passion
Are terrible; yet, though these arguments seem just,
Your whole case will not bear a closer scrutiny.
Though before crowds I am no clever orator,
Among a few, my equals, I can show more skill.
And this is natural; for those speakers who appear
As fools among wise men, the crowd finds eloquent.
But now, faced with this peril, I'm compelled to let
My tongue speak boldly. And I'll answer first that charge
Which you brought first, supposing it would leave me
     shattered
And speechless. Look – you see this sunlight and this earth:
In them there is no man – deny it as you may –
Whose nature is more pure than mine. First, I have learnt
To revere the gods, and to choose friends who undertake
No villainy, whose honour will forbid them make
Vicious requests to those who know them, or respond
With shameful favours; nor am I one, father, to mock
Those that I live with – I am the same man to my friends
Absent or near. Next, that particular act, in which
You think you have caught me, is one that I have never
     touched;
My body is innocent to this day of sexual love.
Except by hearsay, or from pictures I have seen –

Which I have little urge to look at, since my mind
Is virgin still — I do not know this act. It seems
My chastity does not convince you. In that case
It is for you to show what cause corrupted me.
Was Phaedra the most beautiful of all women?
Or did I hope, by union with your legal heir,
To become master in your house? Any such hope
Would be less vain than mentally deranged. Do you think
A throne carries attraction for a balanced mind?
None; since to feel delight in kingship is to be
Corrupted by it.[21] No; my wish is to come first
In the Greek Games, in politics take second place,
Secure in happiness, with the noblest for my friends.
Thus scope for action is assured, while to be free
From danger confers privilege greater than the throne.

You have heard now all I have to say, except one thing:
Had I a witness here to vouch my innocence,
And were your wife but living as I plead my cause,
Then your investigation of events would show
Where the guilt lies. As it is, I swear to you by Zeus,
Guardian of oaths, and by this earth: I never touched
Your wife, nor could have wished to, nor have thought of
    it.
May I die a dishonoured, unremembered death,
May neither sea nor land shelter my lifeless flesh,
If there is sin in me! What fear it was that drove
Phaedra to take her life, I do not know. To speak
Further than this I have no right. Phaedra preserved
Chastity, not possessing the virtue of chastity; I
Possess it, and have practised it to my own hurt.
CHORUS: What you have said will surely clear you of this
    charge;
The weighty sanction of your oath must be believed.
THESEUS: Is this man not a spellmonger, a juggling cheat,
Sure of his power to dominate my spirit with his

Smooth temper, after dishonouring his own father?

HIPPOLYTUS: It is *your* smooth temper, father, that I wonder
at.

If you were my son, I your father, I would not
Have corrected you with exile, I'd have seen you dead
If you'd thought fit to lay a finger on my wife.

THESEUS: Your words are worthy of you! You shall not die
that way —
According to the law you've laid down for yourself.
Many an outcast would be glad of a quick death.
No, you shall wander exiled from your native land
And drain on alien soil the bitter lees of life.

HIPPOLYTUS: What? You will do that? Will you not let Time
present
His evidence in my case, but drive me out today?

THESEUS: Yes, past the Black Sea, past the Atlantic boundary,
Had I the power — so loathsome is the sight of you.

HIPPOLYTUS: You accept no oath, pledge, or prophetic
utterance —
Reject all these, and banish me from home unjudged?

THESEUS: This letter here's no augurer's riddle, but a clear
Convincing charge; and as for prophecy from birds
Flying overhead — to me that means nothing at all.

HIPPOLYTUS: Oh, why do I not unlock my lips? It is through
you,
Gods, whom my silence honours, that I am perishing.
I will not; no words of mine could win belief where most
I need it. I should violate my oath in vain.

THESEUS: Your insufferable piety chokes me to death.
What are you waiting for? Out of my land, I say!

HIPPOLYTUS: Where can I turn, in such a plight? Which of
my friends
Will bid me welcome, banished on a charge like this?

THESEUS: Anyone who delights to entertain as guest
The wife-defiler, expert in foul housekeeping.

HIPPOLYTUS: That wounds me deeply. Oh, it is time indeed
for tears
    If I am seen as foul, and you too think me so.
THESEUS: That was the time for tears and wise forethought,
when you
    Cast off all shame to violate your father's wife.
HIPPOLYTUS: O house! Could but your walls cry out and
speak for me,
    To testify if I could be so vile a man!
THESEUS: You appeal to a dumb witness, very prudently;
    The fact alone, without a voice, confirms your guilt.
HIPPOLYTUS: Oh, I could wish to stand apart and view my-
self,
    To shed tears for this hopeless fate that crushes me!
THESEUS: No doubt; you are much more practised in self-
worship than
    In upright living and blameless conduct to your father.
HIPPOLYTUS: My unhappy mother! In what bitterness I was
born!
    May no one that I love experience bastardy!
THESEUS: Away! You men, get hold of him and drag him off.
    You heard me – I pronounced him exiled long ago.
HIPPOLYTUS: It will go hard with any of them that touches
me.
    If you're so minded, push me out with your own hand.
THESEUS: I shall do so, if you will not obey my word.
    Your exile stirs no breath of pity in my heart.
HIPPOLYTUS: It seems my fate is fixed. How sad and cruel,
that I,
    Who know what I know, know no way to utter it.
                    He turns to the statue of ARTEMIS.
Dear goddess, daughter of Leto, in whose company
I have sat at rest, and hunted! I shall live, in truth,
Exiled from glorious Athens. So, farewell, city
And land of Erechtheus; and farewell, Trozen – so rich

In manifold delights of youth. I speak my last
Word to you now, take my last look. Come, then, you lads
Of Trozen who have grown up with me; say good-bye,
And see me to the border. You will never meet
A man whose nature is more pure, more sound, than mine —
Never, though my own father thinks this is not so.

Exit HIPPOLYTUS *with his companions.*

THESEUS *goes into the palace.*

CHORUS: When I reflect that gods are concerned   [*Strophe*
    for human life,
This thought brings relief in a time of trouble.
Yet, though deep within me
I cherish hope of a kind of understanding,
I am baffled when I survey the mortal scene —
On the one hand men's fortunes, on the other their deeds.
Change follows change,
Coming now from this side, now from that;
Men's lives are uprooted, wandering is endless.

May destiny, in answer to my prayer,   [*Antistrophe*
Grant me from the gods this request:
Fortune that brings well-being,
And a heart untouched by pain.
May the thoughts and resolves of my heart
Be neither stubborn nor false-faced,
My will ready each day
To adapt or change its ways to tomorrow's need,
And share tomorrow's blessing.

My mind is no longer clear;   [*Strophe*
What I see is not what I expected.
For the brightest star of Athena's city
We have seen, we have seen driven out by his father's anger
To look for another country.
O sandy shore fringing the city-wall,

O forest of mountain oaks,
Where in the train of the immortal Huntress
He followed with swift-footed hounds to make his kill!

No more will you mount, Hippolytus,   [Antistrophe
Behind your yoked Thessalian team
Holding the track round the shore-marshes
With the tense drumming of hooves. [22]
The music that sang unsleeping from chords of the curved
    lyre
Shall cease in your father's palace.
There will be no garlands now
In the deep spring grass where Artemis rests;
And by your banishment peace falls
On the rivalry of girls for your bridal bed.

I too at your pitiful fate   [Epode
Shall spend my sad life in tears.
Lost is the joy for which your mother bore you in sorrow.
Oh, I rage at the gods;
Do you hear, do you hear, you sister Graces?
Why do you send him, guiltless of these disasters,
Out of his father's land, away from his home?

CHORUS: Look! I see someone running towards the palace.
    Yes,
    It's one of Hippolytus' servants – breathless, horror-struck!
            Enter MESSENGER.
MESSENGER: Women, where can I find the king? Where is
    Theseus?
    If you know, tell me quickly. Is he in the palace?
CHORUS: Here is the king; he is coming out of the palace now.
            Enter THESEUS.
MESSENGER: Theseus, I come with news of grave concern –
    for you,

And for all our citizens, whether of Athens or Trozen.

THESEUS: What is it? Has some new or worse disaster fallen
    To vex these neighbour cities?

MESSENGER: Sir, Hippolytus
    Is dead, or dying; balanced between life and death.

THESEUS: Who struck him? Did some man take a dislike to
    him
    Whose wife he had assaulted as he did his father's?

MESSENGER: It was his own chariot and team that killed him,
    and
    The curses which your lips called down on your own son
    When you prayed to your father who commands the sea.

THESEUS: You gods! — Why, then, Poseidon, you must be in
    truth
    My father, since you heard and ratified my curse.
    How did he meet his fate, then? Speak, how did the trap
    Of Justice close to crush the man who shamed my bed?

MESSENGER: We were all on the shore beside the breaking
    waves,
    Combing the horses' manes, rubbing them down; and tears
    Were flowing, for word had reached us that Hippolytus
    Was free no more to come and go in Trozen, since
    You had condemned him to the pains of banishment.
    He came to us there, bringing the same tale of tears;
    And a great troop of young men, friends and followers,
    Came with him. After a while he stopped weeping, and said,
    'Enough of folly. My father's word must be obeyed.
    Men, yoke my horses, harness them to the chariot;
    This city of Trozen is no longer my city.'
    Then every man made haste, and quicker than you could say
    it
    We had them harnessed, and set them at the prince's side.
    He caught the reins up from the rail, and with one bound,
    Feet firmly in the footstalls,[23] he stood ready. And first
    He raised his hands to heaven and prayed, 'Zeus, may I die

If I am a guilty man; and may my father learn –
Whether I die or live – the wrong he does to me!'
    And now he had gripped the sharp goad and was plying it
To keep the horses level. We servants began running
Close by the bridles, to escort our master along
The direct road to Argos and Epidauria.
Soon we were striking into the uninhabited tract
Beyond our frontier, where a headland faces towards
What is, by then, the Saronic Gulf. And it was here
That a kind of rumbling underground, like Zeus's thunder,
Rose with a deep roar that was horrible to hear.
The horses upped their heads, pricked ears; a wild panic
Seized on us all – where could the sound be coming from?
We looked out to the breaking surf, and there we saw,
Rearing to the sky, a wave of supernatural size;
It hid from view not only the Scironian cliff
But the whole Isthmus and Asclepius' Rock. And then,
Swelling still huger, spattering foam on every side,
It rushed seething and hissing to the shore, and straight
Towards the four-horse chariot. And in the very moment
Of bursting and crashing, the wave threw forth a monstrous
    savage
Bull, whose bellowing filled the whole earth, which roared
    back
An appalling echo; while, as we watched, the sight was too
Tremendous for any eyes to bear. At once a frenzy
Of terror seized the horses. Hippolytus, being long
Familiar with the animals' nature, gripped the reins
And pulled, leaning his whole weight backward on the straps
Like a sailor tugging at his oar. It was no use;
The horses took the wrought-iron bits between their teeth
And careered on, as though the driver's hand, the reins,
The harness, the heavy chariot, were nothing at all.
When he struggled to steer their hurtling course towards
The soft grass, there was the bull in front to send all four

Crazy with terror and turn them back. But when they went
Insanely tearing towards the rocks, then the bull kept
Close at their side, silent, swerving right in upon
The handrail, till the moment when he crashed the wheel
On a boulder, and spun the chariot tossing in the air.

Then there was wild confusion – wheel-naves, axle, bolts,
All leaping high. Hippolytus, tangled in the reins,
Strung fast in an inextricable knot, was dragged
Along, his head dashed on the rocks, his flesh mangled;
While in a voice terrible to hear he shouted, 'Stop!
You were reared in my own stables – don't grind me to
    death! –
Oh, father, your unpitying curse! – Will no one come
To help an innocent man?' Many indeed were willing;
We ran – but we were left behind. Then he fell clear
At last – I don't know how – from the reins that fettered
    him.
There was little life left in him; he still breathed. The horses
Had vanished – so had that dreadful prodigy of a bull –
Away over the rocky ground, no one knows where.

My lord, I am only one of your palace slaves; but I
Cannot and never will believe your son was guilty
Of such an act; no, not if the whole race of women
Should hang themselves, not if a mountain of such letters
Accused him. I know Hippolytus is a good man.

CHORUS: The wheel has turned; disaster follows on disaster.
Fate is irresistible, and there is no escape.

THESEUS: Because the man who has suffered this had earned
    my hate,
At first your story pleased me. But I revere the gods;
And I remember that he is my son. Therefore
What has happened moves me neither with pleasure nor
    with grief.

MESSENGER: What, then? Are we to bring his shattered body
    here?

Or what would please you? Consider: your son is struck
   down.
Listen to my advice; do not be harsh to him.

THESEUS: Bring him to me. I will see face to face the man
Who told me he did not defile my bed; so that
My words and the heavy hand of heaven may prove his
   guilt.

Exit MESSENGER.

The CHORUS *turn to face the statue of* APHRODITE.

CHORUS: You, Aphrodite, lead captive
The stubborn hearts of gods and of mortals;
At your side bright-wing'd Eros
With flashing flight encircles them.
Love hovers over earth
And over the salt sea's clear song.
When on the maddened spirit
He swoops with sweet enchantment,
Whelps of the mountain know the power of his golden wing;
Fish, and all beasts that draw
Life from the earth's breast, warmth from the sun's eye —
Yes, and the hearts of men,
Yield to the universal spell.
Aphrodite, you alone
Reign in power and honour,
Queen of all creation!

ARTEMIS *appears above her own statue on the other side*
of the stage. As she speaks all turn to her.

ARTEMIS: Theseus, royal son of Aegeus, I command you,
Listen! It is Artemis, Leto's daughter, who speaks.
Why do you, wretch, rejoice at what has happened?
You have killed your son — a most unholy act.
You believed your wife's lies without witness; now
Witness the world how you reap your own undoing!
Will you not cower shamed in the depths of hell?
Soar to the sky to escape this chain of misery?

In the common life of good men there is now
No place for you.

Hear the true state, Theseus, of your unhappy life.
True, it will do no good — but I shall cause you pain.
I came here for this purpose, to disclose your son's
Uprightness of heart, that he may die with a good name;
And to reveal your wife's wild passion — or in some sense
Her nobleness. For Phaedra, plagued and goaded by
That goddess whom I, and all who prize virginity,
Most hate — Phaedra desired your son. Her reason struggled
To subdue passion. Schemes plotted against her will
Led to her death: her nurse informed Hippolytus
Of her affliction, under oath of secrecy.
He honourably resisted her persuasions; even
When you so wronged him, still for reverence of the gods
He would not then revoke his oath. But she, dreading
Exposure, wrote that lying letter and destroyed
Your son with a false tale which you, Theseus, believed.

THESEUS: My son, my son!

ARTEMIS: Do my words hurt you, Theseus? Listen patiently
To what followed — for you have more to suffer yet.
You know your father promised you fulfilment of
Three curses: one you have used most wickedly against
Your own son, when you could have cursed an enemy.
Your father, then, the sea-god, gave you in all good will,
Since he had agreed, no more than he was bound to give;
But you stand guilty of wrong to him, and to me too.
You sought no proof, waited for no prophetic word,
You allowed no room for question or the slow scrutiny
Of time, but with unrighteous haste you flung your curse
And killed your son.

THESEUS: Divine Artemis, let me die!

ARTEMIS: Your sin is great; yet even for this you may yet find
Pardon. For Aphrodite willed all this to happen
To appease her anger; and this law holds among gods,

That none seeks to oppose another's purpose; rather
We stand aloof. I tell you, but that I fear Zeus,
I never would have submitted to the ignominy
Of seeing the man whom, of all mortals, I loved best
Go to his death. But your sin is exempted from
The deepest guilt, first, by your ignorance of the facts;
Then, by her death your wife prevented any test
Of what she alleged, and so made sure of your belief.

    This day's disaster, then, has burst chiefly upon you;
But I too suffer; for it is no joy to gods
When good men die. But mark you: men of evil ways,
Their house, their children – all we utterly destroy.

HIPPOLYTUS *is seen approaching, supported by his servants.*

CHORUS: Ah, look! Here comes the piteous prince,
  His young flesh torn, his fair head bruised.
  Ah, suffering house! What grief is fulfilled for you,
  Twice struck by the hand of heaven!

HIPPOLYTUS: Weep for me, weep for me,
  Scarred, broken, trampled under foot
  By man and god alike unjust –
  My father's curse, Poseidon's power;
  Weep for my death!
  My forehead is pierced with the fierce pain,
  My brain convulsed with the pulse of anguish.
  Enough now, I am fainting; let me rest.
  O horses my own hand fed,
  Your cursed strength has crushed and killed me.
  Men, for god's sake have careful hands
  And touch me gently where the flesh is raw.
  Lift me, lead me softly, with a steady grip.
  Doomed, fallen, cursed by my father's fault –
  Zeus, do you see my agony?
  I, whose life was holy, I who revered the gods,
  Who surpassed all others in purity,
  Now tread my way to the dark, seeing death before me,

My life lost, and all that it held, lost;
All my care and striving
To live in piety towards others –
All unrequited, all lost.
Oh, oh, oh! It comes on me now – pain, pain!
Let go, let me go,
And let death come to heal me.
Oh, for pity's sake, kill me, finish me off!
I long for a rending spear
To cut me apart and lay my life to rest.
Now through your fatal curse, my father,
The hellish heritage of bloodguiltiness
Won by forgotten ancestors
Impatient bursts its bounds
And descends on me – why? why?
I am guilty of no wrong!
O endless misery! What shall I say?
How can I free my life from suffering
And forget pain?

> *Servants bring a couch from the palace*
> *and lay him on it.*

Come, black irresistible darkness,
Come in your cruelty
And lay me to sleep in death.

ARTEMIS: I pity you, poor soul, galled by a bitter yoke.
It was your nobleness of heart that caused your death.

HIPPOLYTUS: Ah! Breath of divine fragrance! Out of my despair
I hear you, goddess, and my tormented body rests.
– She is here! The goddess Artemis is in this place.

ARTEMIS: Yes, she is here – to you the dearest of all gods.

HIPPOLYTUS: Divine mistress, you see my miserable state?

ARTEMIS: I see it; but my eyes are forbidden to shed tears.

HIPPOLYTUS: Where is your huntsman? You have no attendant now.

ARTEMIS: It is too true; your death takes from me a dear friend.

HIPPOLYTUS: No one to graze your horses, guard your images.

ARTEMIS: The unscrupulous Aphrodite planned this day's events.

HIPPOLYTUS: Ah! Then I understand what god has ruined me.

ARTEMIS: She resented your neglect, disliked your purity.

HIPPOLYTUS: She has destroyed all three of us; I see it now.

ARTEMIS: All three – your father, and you, and your father's wife.

HIPPOLYTUS: My father suffers deeply, and I weep for him.

ARTEMIS: Duped by the machinations of a deity!

HIPPOLYTUS: Father, what cruel misfortune strikes at you today!

THESEUS: My son, my heart is broken; life is loathsome to me.

HIPPOLYTUS: I grieve for you, though guilty, more than for myself.

THESEUS: If only, my son, I could die in place of you!

HIPPOLYTUS: Poseidon's gifts brought little joy to you, his son.

THESEUS: His gift? O that his name had never passed my lips!

HIPPOLYTUS: What then? You would have killed me, you were so enraged.

THESEUS: The gods' deceptions lured me out of my right mind.

HIPPOLYTUS: Oh, if gods were but subject to a mortal's curse!

ARTEMIS: Let be. Though you lie in the dark of earth, that wrong
Which Aphrodite's angry purpose wreaked on you
Shall be repaid, to vindicate your piety
And noble spirit. I will requite her, striking down
Myself, with this unfailing bow, whatever man
Her heart holds dearest in the world. On you, poor youth,

I will bestow, in solace for your suffering,
High ritual honours in the city of Trozen.
Unmarried virgins shall, before their wedding, shear
Their tresses in your memory; age after age
A rich harvest of tears and mourning shall be yours,
And maidens' skill in music flow perpetually
To tell your story. Phaedra too shall give her name
To memory, and songs recall her love for you.

Son of old Aegeus, take your own son in your arms
And clasp him to your heart. It was in ignorance
You killed him. Men may well sin, when gods so ordain.

Hippolytus, I commend you not to hate your father;
This doom by which you perish was apportioned you.
So now farewell. I may not look upon the dead,
Nor stain my sight with the anguish of departing breath;
And I observe you are already near your end.

HIPPOLYTUS: Farewell! Depart to blessedness, immortal
maid.

How easily you leave our long companionship!
At your desire I end all hatred for my father,
As in the past I have been obedient to your words.

Exit ARTEMIS.

Ah! Darkness has reached me, closing on my eyes.
Father, take hold of me, compose my limbs.

THESEUS: Dear son,
What are you doing to me? Will you break my heart?

HIPPOLYTUS: I see before me now the gates of the dead
world.

THESEUS: And will you leave me guilty, with unholy hands?

HIPPOLYTUS: No, you are free. I here absolve you of my
death.

THESEUS: I am free? You discharge me of bloodguiltiness?

HIPPOLYTUS: I swear it by the conquering bow of Artemis.

THESEUS: O dearest son, how noble a heart you show your
father!

HIPPOLYTUS: Pray that your true-born sons show you such
    nobleness.
THESEUS: O generous soul, dying in honest innocence!
HIPPOLYTUS: Farewell, father, farewell, farewell!
THESEUS: Dear son, do not forsake me. Courage, my son!
HIPPOLYTUS: My time for courage is past. I am gone, father.
    Cover my face now quickly with my cloak.
THESEUS: Frontiers of famous Athens, land of Pallas,
    How you will feel this loss! How often, Aphrodite,
    Shall I in tears remember the wrong that you have done!

> THESEUS *goes into the palace followed by servants*
> *bearing the body of* HIPPOLYTUS.

CHORUS: This sorrow, common to all citizens,
    Has fallen upon us unforeseen.
    In ritual mourning many tears will flow;
    For when great men die
    Their remembered story stirs the greater grief.[24]

IPHIGENIA
IN
TAURIS

CHARACTERS

IPHIGENIA, *daughter of Agamemnon*
ORESTES, *her brother*
PYLADES, *his cousin and friend*
THOAS, *king of the Taurians*
HERDSMAN
MESSENGER
The Goddess ATHENA
CHORUS *of captive Greek women
attending Iphigenia*
SOLDIERS *attending Thoas*

Scene: The forecourt of the temple of Artemis on the Taurian coast, near the western end of the Crimean Peninsula. An altar is visible.

Enter IPHIGENIA *from the temple.*

IPHIGENIA: I am Iphigenia. I am descended from
Pelops the son of Tantalus, who drove his swift
Chariot to Pisa and there won Hippodamia,
Oenomaus' daughter, as his bride. From her he got
Atreus, whose sons were Menelaus and Agamemnon.
Agamemnon was my father; and Tyndareos' daughter
My mother, Clytemnestra. Yes, I am that same
Iphigenia whom, beside the eddying swirl
Where restless winds churn dark Euripus[1] to and fro,
My father sacrificed, for Helen's sake – or so
It is thought – to Artemis, in the famous land-locked bay
Of Aulis. There King Agamemnon had assembled
His great fleet of a thousand Hellene ships, resolved
To crown the Achaean arms in triumph over Troy,
And thus to gratify Menelaus by exacting
Revenge for the insolent seizure of his wife Helen.

But fearful storms, penning his fleet in port,[2] drove him
To enquiry through burnt-offerings; and Calchas[3] pro-
nounced:
'Agamemnon, ruler of this Hellene armament,
You shall see no ship sail till Artemis receive
Your daughter Iphigenia's blood in sacrifice.
Once, long ago,[4] you vowed to Artemis, bringer of light,
The loveliest creature born within twelve months. Your
own
Wife Clytemnestra has a child' – awarding me
This prize of beauty; – 'her, then, you must sacrifice.'

On a false pretext, which Odysseus fabricated,
That I was to be Achilles' bride, they stole me from

My mother. I came to Aulis. There they held me high
Over the altar. As the sword fell, Artemis
Snatched me from death, gave the Achaeans in my place
A deer, and brought me through the bright air to make my
    home
Here in this Taurian country, where a barbaric king
Rules a barbaric people – Thoas, who won his name,
A runner's name, from the wing-like swiftness of his feet.
    The goddess made me priestess in her temple here;
And at her feast – so-called, a pleasant name for rites
Which Artemis takes pleasure in; the acts performed
I do not speak of, since I fear her deity;
For, by a custom that held here before I came,[5]
I offer all Hellenes who set foot on this shore –
At this feast of the goddess I begin the rites;
The sacrifice itself is an unspoken act
Performed by others in the interior of the shrine.
    Last night brought me strange dreams. I'll purge them
        forth in words
Now to the open sky, in hope to ease my heart.
I dreamt I had escaped out of this land, and lived
In Argos. There I and my maidens were asleep,
When the earth's shoulders heaved and shook. I flew out-
    doors,
And stood and watched walls, coping, roof, and the whole
    house
Reel at one blow and crash to earth. Out of the ruin
Which was my father's house, it seemed, one column stood;
Brown hair flowed from its head, it spoke with human voice.
And I performed for it this deadly ritual
For strangers, sprinkling water as on one destined
To die, and weeping. I interpret the dream thus:
It was Orestes I prepared for death; and he
Has died. For what are pillars of a house? Its sons.
And those whose heads I touch with lustral water die.

So now I want to pour libations for my brother —
All I have power to do, being so far away.
My maids must help — women of Hellas whom the king
Appoints to serve me. Why are they not yet here? I'll go
Into the house — this temple of Artemis — my home!

>   IPHIGENIA *goes into the temple.*
>   *Enter* ORESTES *and* PYLADES *from the shore.*

ORESTES: Look, here's a path. Watch now, there may be someone near.

PYLADES: I see, yes; and I'm keeping watch on every side.

ORESTES: Pylades, is this, do you think, the temple of Artemis,
The place we've come from Argos over the sea to find?

PYLADES: It surely must be, Orestes. Don't you think the same?

ORESTES: And there — do you see the altar stained with Hellene blood?

PYLADES: Why, yes — those brownish streaks like locks of hair — they're blood!

ORESTES: Do you see, hung high up under the coping — those are spoils!

PYLADES: They are — trophies of visitors who perished here.
Well, we must keep our eyes and wits alert all round.

ORESTES: O Phoebus,[6] where has your oracle led me once again?
I obeyed you; I avenged my father's death, and killed
My mother. Since then I am an outcast, haled and harried
This way and that, hounded by Furies to and fro,
Always in flight. I have had my share of suffering!
I came and asked you how I could reach the end of this
Whirlwheel of madness which drove me with torment through
The length of Hellas. You told me to come to this
Taurian country, where your sister Artemis
Is worshipped, and to take her statue which, they say,

Fell from the sky into this temple; to possess it
By craft or luck in face of every peril, and then
Give it to Athens – that was what you said, no more;
When I had done it, then I should have a breathing-space
From pain. I have obeyed you. Here I am, in this
Unknown, unwelcoming country.

                              Advise me, Pylades –
You share this enterprise with me – what shall we do?
You see the height of the temple wall; are we to get in
By climbing? They would surely see us. Or we might
Bring crowbars to prize open the bronze bolts – if only
We knew something about them. If we're caught opening
The doors, forcing an entrance, we'll be killed. Let's get
Back to the ship we came in, while we're still alive.

PYLADES: Run away? Out of the question – we're not used to
   it.
We're here at a god's bidding – we can't play the coward.
Let's leave the temple now and hide among those caves
Where the dark tide floods through the cliffs, and well away
From the ship – someone might see it and inform the king,
And we'd be attacked and captured. Then, when murky
   night
Frowns on the world, we must use all the courage, all
The resource we have, to steal that polished statue out
Of the temple. Look: between the triglyphs – there's a space
Big enough to climb through. Come! Good men and difficul-
   ties
Are made to match; a coward's a failure anywhere.
I tell you, we've not rowed our ship this long journey,
And got here, only to turn round and row home again!

ORESTES: You're right, and I must listen to you. Let's find
   some place
Where we can hide. Apollo cannot wilfully
Cause his own oracle to perish unfulfilled.
Bold is the word! We're young, and danger's no excuse.

They steal away towards the shore. Enter the
CHORUS *from the side of the temple.*

CHORUS: Keep holy silence, all whose homes are here
 Beside the Unfriendly Sea,[7]
 Beyond the Clashing Rocks.
 Huntress daughter of Leto,
 Artemis of the mountains,[8]
 I approach your court with ritual steps,
 Virgin slave to your temple's virgin guardian;
 Pass between towering pillars under a roof of gold.
 Far away, by the cool Eurotas,[9]
 Horses of Hellas crop the green meadows
 Between the town wall and the fringe of trees:
 There stood my father's house.

   IPHIGENIA *enters from the central door.*

 We have come. – Oh, what has happened? Why are you sad?
 Daughter of great Agamemnon,
 Who led the famous fleet to the towers of Troy,
 Ships and armed men by thousands and tens of thousands,
 Why did you call us to the temple?
 Why did you send for us?

IPHIGENIA: Oh, my girls!
 I am sunk in bitter tears and deep distress.
 Music is turned to mourning, songs to a tuneless wail.
 For Death lays pain, pain on my inmost heart,
 Blow follows blow, fatal and cruel:
 I weep for the lost life of my own brother.
 Such a sight I saw, such a vision came to me
 In the night whose darkness has just passed.
 My life is shattered and ended,
 My father's house fallen, my family extinct.
 O city, city of Argos, how you have suffered!
 Hear my indignation, you unseen Powers
 Who rob from me and send down to death
 My only brother! For him are these libations

Which I will pour out on the earth's back –
Milk in fountains from the upland herds,
The holy offering of Bacchus' wine,
The toil of tawny bees –
The cup of the dead, set for the soothing of the dark Powers.
Give me the golden bowl
And the offering for the god of death.

Child of Agamemnon's race,
Numbered with the dead below,
Take these holy gifts from me.
I can lay no lock of hair,
Drop no tear, upon your tomb.
From the land that bore us both
Fate has torn me far away;
There men saw me slaughtered,
There men think me buried.

CHORUS: Mistress, we will echo your chant of mourning
With Eastern songs, with wild laments,
Music to move tears for the dead,
Notes the glad heart abhors,
The solemn dirge that Death himself intones.

The heir to Atreus' throne is dead,
Hope of the royal house is dead.
Many a glorious king has Argos known:
Whose is now the sovereignty?
Blow after blow staggers the cursed city
Since that first wickedness[10] at which
The Sun, driving wing'd horses like whirling flames,
Swerved from his course, and averted
The holy glance of his glory.
Agony upon agony, murder upon murder, dread and despair,
Haunted the unhappy house.
Now for the sons of Tantalus killed in time past

Falls vengeance on the last of his line:
What God should abhor, God to your hurt pursues.
IPHIGENIA: From my beginning Fate was ill-fate for me.
From the night my mother loosed her maiden girdle,
From the hour I was conceived, over my childhood
The hand of Fate lay hard.
My unhappy mother, Leda's daughter,[11]
Bore me as first-fruit of her marriage,
Wooed by many princes of Hellas,
But reared as a vowed offering –
A doomed victim of my father's villainy,
A sacrifice empty of rejoicing.
They sent me in a chariot of state to the sands of Aulis,
A mocked and unblessed bride for Achilles son of Thetis.

Now in this bleak exile beside the Inhospitable Sea
I live without husband, child, city, or friend.
I cannot join in the Argive Hymn to Hera;
Not for me to weave in coloured tapestry,
Charmed by the loom's music,
The story of Pallas and the Titans. Instead of this
The rites I celebrate are unfit for song;
I drench an altar with blood of travellers;
I pity them as they lament their fate,
As their tears fall my heart is wrung.

Now let me forget all that; my tears now
Yearn towards Argos and my dead brother.
I left him a little child at my mother's breast,
So young and fresh then, her arms clasping him close:
The prince royal of Argos, Orestes.
CHORUS: But look, my lady – this is one of the king's herds-
    men;
He comes from the sea-shore, and has some news for you.
Enter a HERDSMAN

HERDSMAN: Daughter of Agamemnon and Clytemnestra, listen.

Strange things have happened; I will tell you the whole story.

IPHIGENIA: What is there in your story that excites you so?

HERDSMAN: Why, two young men have come by ship and landed here –

Sailed safely through the blue Symplegades.[12] They'll be
Suitable victims and a pleasing sacrifice
For divine Artemis. So get ready the barley-meal
And holy-water now, as fast as possible.

IPHIGENIA: Does their appearance show what country they are from?

HERDSMAN: They are from Hellas; I know that, but nothing more.

IPHIGENIA: Did you not hear the name of either of these men?

HERDSMAN: I did; one of them called the other Pylades.

IPHIGENIA: And his companion – what was he called? Did you hear?

HERDSMAN: Why, no; we heard no other name, so no one knows.

IPHIGENIA: Then tell me how you saw and encountered them, and how

You caught them.

HERDSMAN: We were right down by the breaking waves –

IPHIGENIA: And what would bring you herdsmen down to the sea-shore?

HERDSMEN: We took our cattle there to wash them in salt water.

IPHIGENIA: Oh, yes. Begin again, then; tell me exactly how
You captured them – that's what I wish to learn. These men
Were long in coming; and the altar of Artemis
Is not yet dyed too deep with streams of Hellene blood.

HERDSMAN: We had brought our cattle down from the wood-
    land pastures, and
    Were driving them towards the sea which flows in through
    The Clashing Rocks. There is a hollow below the cliff,
    Carved out by great waves bursting through, used as a shelter
    By purple-fishers; there one of our drovers saw
    The two young men, and made his way back warily
    On tip-toe. 'Don't you see,' says he, 'those are two gods
    Sitting there.' One of us then, a god-fearing man,
    Held up his hands and, turning towards them, prayed: 'O
        lord
    Palaemon, son of the sea-nymph Leucothea, protector
    Of ships, be gracious to us; or if you are the twin
    Dioscori sitting there, or beings that Nereus loves,
    The father of the fifty immortal ocean-nymphs –
    Be gracious!' But another, a profane, reckless fellow,
    Laughed at his prayer, and said they must be shipwrecked
        men
    Who, knowing our country's custom is to sacrifice
    Strangers, were crouching terrified below the rock.
    Most of us agreed, and said we ought to catch the men
    To sacrifice to Artemis, as our law directs.
        While we were talking, one of them got up from the rock
    And stood there groaning, his head jerking up and down,
    His hands a-tremble – raving mad; and he hallooed
    Like a huntsman: 'Pylades, do you see her? There's another,
    A fiend from Hades – can't you see? Those gaping fangs –
    They're adders reaching out to kill me! There's a third,
    Who breathes out gory flames and fans them with her wings;
    She holds in her arms my mother – a massive rock to fling
    And crush me with! She'll kill me – where can I escape?'
    Well, no such sights were to be seen; but he confused
    The cattle bellowing and the dogs all barking, with
    The similar sounds the Furies are supposed to utter.
        We sat there silent and astonished, ready to act.

Suddenly the man jumped up and drew his sword, and leapt
Like a lion right among our cattle, lunging out
And stabbing them in flank and rib, imagining
That he was fighting off the immortal Furies, till
The shore and the salt water flowered with bloody foam.
So, when we saw the poor beasts being felled and slaughtered,
Every man of us got some weapon; we blew our horns
And called our countrymen to help. Herdsmen, we thought,
Were no match, if it came to a fight, for two well-built
Young foreigners. A good handful of us soon gathered.

By now the man had shaken off his insane fit;
He fell down, dribbling foam over his beard. So we,
Seeing him fallen, seized our chance; each one of us
Pelted or struck with all his might. The second man
Was wiping foam from his friend's lips, supporting him,
Shielding him with the finely-woven cloak he wore,
Watching against the hail of blows, and still intent
On helping and comforting his friend. The first man now
Was sane again. He leapt up from the ground, and saw
A wave of enemies pressing close, and knew that fate
Was upon them, and cried out in despair. We never stopped
The shower of stones; we hemmed them in on every side.

It was then we heard his dread battle-cry: 'Pylades,
We shall die; so let's die nobly! Draw your sword and
    follow.'
Well, when we saw those two swords brandished at our
    heads,
Away we scattered, over the rocks and up the glens.
But if one fled, others attacked with stones; and if
They routed these, those who had fled before renewed
The attack. And here was a marvel: of all the stones we
    threw
Not one struck home, or scarred the goddess's sacrifice!
At last we laid hands on them, not by bravery,
But closing round in a circle till we knocked the swords

Out of their hands with stones, and they sank to their knees
Exhausted. Then we led them to the king; and he,
Soon as he saw them, ordered them to be sent at once
To you for purification and then sacrifice.
You used to pray, my lady,[13] that victims such as these
Should come to you. If you kill men of this quality
Hellas will make amends for what she did to you,
And the sacrifice at Aulis will be avenged in full.

CHORUS: An amazing story! Who can the man be, making this
    Mysterious voyage from Hellas to the Unfriendly Sea?

IPHIGENIA: Enough. Herdsman, go now and bring the men.
    The rites
Ensuing are my concern and I will see to them.

Exit HERDSMAN.

    In past days, O my suffering heart, when Hellene men
Came to your ministrations, you were gentle, full
Of compassion for them, shedding those tears that were due
To your own flesh and blood. But now my dream has made
Me cruel. I think Orestes sees the sun no more;
Then you who have come, whoever you may be, shall find
I am your enemy.

She turns to the CHORUS.

    Friends, here's another truth which I have just perceived.
The unfortunate, meeting those still more unfortunate,
Think of their own hard fate and feel no sympathy.
Zeus never yet sent wind or ship to convey through
The Twin Rocks to this country Helen, who destroyed
My life, or Menelaus, for my just revenge,
To make a second Aulis for atonement here.
Aulis! where Greek hands held me like a calf prepared
For slaughter, my own father playing the part of priest!
I weep again, remembering — how can I forget? —
What happened there; the times I stretched my hand to
    touch
My father's beard, cling to his knees; the things I said —

'This is a shameful marriage you have brought me to –
You, father! At this moment, while you are killing me,
My mother and my friends at home are all singing
The wedding-song for me, and flutes fill the whole house
With music; and I am being put to death by you!
The Achilles you chose for me was not Peleus' son;
Your treacherous chariot brought me here to wed with
    Death –
The grave my bridegroom, and my marriage-token blood!'
At home, I hid my face in my fine wedding-veil,
And would not take my brother in my arms – and he
Is dead now; and I would not kiss my sister's lips,
For I was hot with blushes, going to the house
Of Achilles. I would see Argos again one day,
I said; and I would keep my kisses until then.
    Orestes, dearest brother, what rare dignity
And beauty of life is lost to you, if you are dead!
What splendour of inheritance! – As for Artemis,
I find her guilty of hypocrisy. She calls
Unclean one who has touched blood, or a woman in labour,
Or a corpse, and bars him from her altars; yet herself
Takes pleasure in these offerings of human lives!
Could Zeus beget, and Leto bring to birth, such vile
Folly? Impossible! I do not believe the tale
Of Tantalus' feast – that gods were pleased with a child's
    flesh.
The truth is – men of this country, being murderers,
Impute their sordid practice to divine command.
That any god is evil I do not believe.

              Exit IPHIGENIA *into the temple*

CHORUS: Dim purple rock, where sea flows into   [*Strophe*
        purple sea,
    Gateway from Europe to the lands of Asia,
    Where Io in her mad agony passed through,
    From Argos flying to these friendless waters!

Tell us, who are these men?
What river flows past their forsaken home?
Eurotas, clear between green rushes?
Or the holy stream of Dirce?[14]
Why have they come? come to a sullen land
Where the altar of Artemis daughter of Zeus runs red
And human blood splashes the pillars?

Was it the jealous search for wealth to exalt   [Antistrophe
    their home
That drove their sails racing before the wind,
That plashed their pinewood oars, two wings as one,
To bring home riches over the wide waters?
Such hope is sweet to men;
No mortal sorrow can quench it.
They wander over the waves, visit strange cities,
Winning their weight of wealth,
All alike sure of achievement; yet
One man's guess misses the lucky moment,
Another finds fortune in his lap.

How did they pass the rocks that run together?   [Strophe
How did they pass the unsleeping swell of Phineus' bay?
Then, coasting close to the beach,
Skimming the choppy foam of Amphitrite,
Where the fifty Nereid maidens chant in a circling chorus,
While a breeze bellies the sails
And the rolling rudder sings astern;
As south wind, west wind[15] urges onward
To the coast of myriads of sea-birds, the white shore;
To the smooth course that Achilles made for running –
How did they sail so far over the hostile sea?
I pray the prayer my mistress prayed: that   [Antistrophe
    Helen,
Leda's darling child, might chance to come

From Troy to this shore, to receive
Round her long hair the garland of water-drops
Before the blood flows, and to die,
Her throat severed by my mistress's hand
In just reprisal! But, of all news,
The most welcome would be this – if a ship from Hellas
Came to free me from this weary slavery.
I long to see once more, even in a dream,
My father's house and city; to taste again
The delight of singing together
Which joins the hearts of rich and poor.

CHORUS: Look! The two men, with their hands fast bound,
Are coming – fresh blood for the altar of Artemis;
Keep silence, friends. – That herdsman told no lie:
Here to the temple come the choicest manhood of Hellas!
– Goddess, if this barbaric country's ritual
Pleases your heart, accept their sacrifice –
An offering which the laws of Hellas
Teach us to call abhorrent.[16]

Enter ORESTES *and* PYLADES, *guarded;*
also IPHIGENIA *from the temple.*

IPHIGENIA: Come. My first care is that the rites of Artemis
Be duly ordered. So untie the strangers' arms;
They must now stand unfettered, being consecrate.
Next, go into the temple and prepare whatever
Custom and the observance of this rite demand.

The guards go in. IPHIGENIA, *alone with* ORESTES *and*
PYLADES, *gives a deep sigh.*

You were once little children: who was your mother then?
Your father? Had you a sister? It is sad for her
To lose so fine a pair of brothers. Such chances –
Who knows to whose lot they will fall? The ways of gods
Move to invisible ends; the next calamity
Is not revealed; events mislead and baffle us.

Tell me what place you come from, O unhappy men!
You are the first to come for a long time; and long
You'll be away from home, below the earth – for ever.

ORESTES: Lady, whoever you may be, why grieve like this,
And make more bitter to us our approaching fate?
He is not a wise man who, in sight of death, attempts
To quell the fear of death, when there's no hope of life,
By seeking pity. Out of one evil he makes two:
He's known for a fool, and he dies none the less. Let Chance
Take its own course. We need no tears from you. We know
And understand what sacrifices take place here.

IPHIGENIA: One of you on the shore just now was named by
    the other
Pylades. Which is he? I wish to know this first.

ORESTES: If learning this gives you some pleasure – it is he.

IPHIGENIA: Of what Greek city was he born a citizen?

ORESTES: What profit would it bring you, lady, to know that?

IPHIGENIA: Are you two brothers? Did one mother bear you
    both?

ORESTES: We are brothers in love, lady; but not by blood.

IPHIGENIA: And what name did your father give you at your
    birth?

ORESTES: To name me justly – I am called The Unfortunate.

IPHIGENIA: Ascribe that name to Fortune; that is not what I
    ask.

ORESTES: I will die nameless and be safe from mockery.

IPHIGENIA: Why do you grudge this? Is your pride so reso-
    lute?

ORESTES: My body is yours; you shall not sacrifice my name.

IPHIGENIA: Will you not even tell me what your city is?

ORESTES: To answer will not help me, since I am to die.

IPHIGENIA: I ask a favour. What prevents you granting it?

ORESTES: Then – I claim famous Argos as my father's city.

IPHIGENIA: What? You were born in Argos? That's the
    truth?

ORESTES: It is.
  I come from the once proud and prosperous Mycenae.

IPHIGENIA: Are you an exile from your country? What
    happened?

ORESTES: Yes, in one sense a willing exile; yet not willing.

IPHIGENIA: You are the visitor I have longed for – one from
    Argos!

ORESTES: Then hug your good luck; it's no answer to *my*
    prayers.

IPHIGENIA: Would you answer a question that I long to
    ask?

ORESTES: Why not? It makes no difference to my present
    plight.

IPHIGENIA: The name of Troy is in the world's mouth: you
    know it?

ORESTES: I wish I did not – had not even dreamt of it.

IPHIGENIA: They say that Troy no longer stands, but was laid
    waste
    In war.

ORESTES: That is so. Your informant was correct.

IPHIGENIA: And Helen [17] – has she gone back to Menelaus's
    house?

ORESTES: She has – and brought a curse with her for one I
    know.

IPHIGENIA: Where is she? I too have a score to settle with
    her.

ORESTES: In Sparta, re-united with her first husband.

IPHIGENIA: She is loathed by every Hellene, not by me alone.

ORESTES: I too have reaped the harvest of her marriages.

IPHIGENIA: The Achaean army, then, returned, as is re-
    ported?

ORESTES: Ha! There you ask me the whole story in one word.

IPHIGENIA: I want to share that story with you before you
    die.

ORESTES: Since you desire it, question me; I'll answer you.

IPHIGENIA: Did a certain priest, Calchas, ever return from Troy?

ORESTES: No, he is dead – so they were saying in Mycenae.

IPHIGENIA: Artemis, you did well! – And Odysseus, what of him?

ORESTES: He has not reached home yet, but is still alive, they say.

IPHIGENIA: I hope he will die, and never reach his home again.

ORESTES: Don't curse him; he is oppressed with every kind of trouble.

IPHIGENIA: And is the Nereid's son, Achilles, still alive?

ORESTES: He is not; and his marriage at Aulis came to nothing.

IPHIGENIA: Nothing but treachery, as those who suffered know.

ORESTES: Who are you, asking these apt questions about Hellas?

IPHIGENIA: That was my home. I died there when I was a child.

ORESTES: Then it is natural, lady, that you long for news.

IPHIGENIA: What does report say of the successful general?

ORESTES: Who? That description does not fit the man I knew.

IPHIGENIA: I mean the king they called Agamemnon, Atreus' son.

ORESTES: I don't know. Lady, no more questions about him!

IPHIGENIA: Friend, don't refuse, I beg you; give me this pleasure.

ORESTES: He is dead; and his sad death destroyed another life.

IPHIGENIA: Not dead? What happened to him? Oh! What misery!

ORESTES: Why do you weep for him? Was he related to you?

IPHIGENIA: The memory of his former greatness makes me weep.

ORESTES: His end was terrible. His own wife struck him dead.

IPHIGENIA: How pitiful! – for her who killed, for him no less
Who died. [18]

ORESTES: Now stop your questions, ask me nothing more.

IPHIGENIA: Tell me just this: the dead king's wife – does she
still live?

ORESTES: She does not. Her son killed her – yes, her very
son.

IPHIGENIA: O house of misery and madness! Why did he – ?

ORESTES: He exacted vengeance for his father, whom she
killed.

IPHIGENIA: How rightly done! – How evil! – Yet revenge was
just.

ORESTES: His justice wins no recognition from the gods.

IPHIGENIA: Does any of the king's children still live in his
house?

ORESTES: His death left only a daughter, Electra, still at
home.

IPHIGENIA: What is said of the daughter who was sacrificed?

ORESTES: Nothing, but that she died, and now does not exist.

IPHIGENIA: She is to be pitied; so is he who killed his child.

ORESTES: Her blood was the unjust ransom for a worthless
wife.

IPHIGENIA: The dead king's son – is he in Argos, and alive?

ORESTES: He lives a wretched life, nowhere and everywhere.

IPHIGENIA: He lives! So much for my false dreams – they
mean nothing. [19]

ORESTES: You are right. The gods themselves, even those we
call prophetic,
Are no more trustworthy than fleeting dreams. The world
Of gods is as chaotic as our mortal world.
What galls one is that, while still of sound mind, he should,
By heeding the words of prophets, plunge himself into
A depth of ruin only experience can fathom.

CHORUS: And what of us? [20] Do we not know what sorrow is?
Our parents too were dear to us; where are they now?

And living, or not living? Who can tell us this?

IPHIGENIA: Friends, listen: a thought has come to me. Some
   good follows
Most often when the same plan pleases everyone.
Would you be willing, if I save your life, to take
A message to my friends in Argos, and to carry
A letter, which a prisoner once wrote for me? [21]
He pitied me, and saw that my hand was not guilty,
But that he died under the law of Artemis,
Who judged it right. Since then, I have had no one who
Could be my messenger to Argos, buy his life
By carrying my letter to – one dear to me.
You seem to be no enemy to me, [22] and you know
Mycenae; save your life, then, and go back – where I
Would go too! The reward you win brings no disgrace;
You bear one little letter, and you gain your life.
And since this city's law demands a victim, let
Your friend alone be sacrificed to Artemis.

ORESTES: All you have said, lady, is well, except one thing:
To let my friend die would be more than I could bear.
Our voyage, with all its dangers, is *my* enterprise;
He came only to share what I must needs endure.
For me to purchase favour with his life, and free
Myself from peril, is not right. Let it be thus:
Give him the letter; he will take it to Argos, and
Deliver it to your satisfaction. My own life
Is his who wants it. If a man, to escape himself,
Will run his friend's neck into the noose, [23] he is a coward.
This man's my friend; I value his life as my own.

IPHIGENIA: O generous heart, so true in friendship! You are
   sprung
Surely from royal stock. I pray that the one man
Left of my family may be like you. I too,
Friends, have a brother – if one 'has' what one never sees.
So, since you thus prefer it, we will send your friend

To bear my letter, and you shall die. This is a strange
Eagerness that possesses you to stay and die!

ORESTES: Whose fearful function will it be to offer me?

IPHIGENIA: Mine; Artemis entrusts this office to my care.

ORESTES: A tragic lot, young woman, and unenviable.

IPHIGENIA: I live under necessity, which I must heed.

ORESTES: Do you yourself, a woman, kill men with the
    sword?

IPHIGENIA: No; I cast water on your head for purifying.

ORESTES: And who will be my slaughterer? May I ask this?

IPHIGENIA: Inside the temple there are those whose care it is.

ORESTES: What kind of tomb will welcome me when I am
    dead?

IPHIGENIA: The sacred fire within; then a broad cleft of rock.

ORESTES: Great gods! If but my sister's hand might wrap my
    limbs
    For burial!

IPHIGENIA: Whoever you are, unhappy man,
    Your prayer is vain. She lives far from this savage place.
    Yet, since you are from Argos, I will not neglect
    To do for you all that is possible. I will heap
    Rich gifts above your grave, spill golden olive-oil
    To quench your ashes, pour over your pyre the bright
    Liquor which yellow bees sip from the hillside flowers.
    I will go now and fetch my letter from the temple.
    For what I do, do not think *me* your enemy.

The guards re-appear.

    You temple-servants, guard them, leaving them unbound.
    [*To herself*] Now, it may be, I can send word, beyond all hope,
    To Argos, to one dearer than all other friends.
    My letter, telling him that one he thought was dead
    Still lives, will speak, and crown his joy with certainty!

Exit IPHIGENIA.

CHORUS: I grieve for you, whose blood
    The sprinkling of holy water soon will claim.

ORESTES: This is no cause for pity; but farewell, good friends.

CHORUS: Pylades, favoured by fortune, we rejoice with you;
In time you will set foot on your native soil.

PYLADES: This is no cause for joy, when death parts friend
from friend.

CHORUS (to PYLADES): A voyage of tears awaits you.
        (to ORESTES): Pitiful death awaits you.
Which is the more bitter, life or death?
My heart is dazed and doubtful: for which fate
Should my grief cry louder?

ORESTES: Gods! Have you the same thought that I have,
Pylades?

PYLADES: I don't know. I am lost for words. What is your
thought?

ORESTES: Who is that woman? The way she questioned us
about
The war at Troy, the Achaeans' homecoming, and that old
Bird-watcher Calchas — she's a true Hellene! She named
Achilles; and how pitifully she asked about
Agamemnon and his wife and children! She must be
An Argive born, or she would never want to send
A letter, or enquire in such detail, as if
Her life depended on the city's well-being.

PYLADES: You have said what I was just about to say, except
For this: the story of the two kings is known and told
Wherever travellers go. No; something else she said —

ORESTES: What, then? Something you didn't understand?
Tell me.

PYLADES: For me to live when you are killed is a disgrace.
I shared your voyage here; it's for me to share your death.
If I sail home, in Argos and the Phocian valleys
I shall be called coward and traitor. There's no lack
Of evil minds. Most men will say that I betrayed
You, and came safely home alone; or even that I
Killed you, taking advantage of your family troubles

To plot against you and gain your throne as lawful heir,
Being your sister's husband. This thought turns me sick
With fear and shame. I am your friend, and have no choice:
To avoid slander, I must breathe my last with you,
And give my body, with yours, to the knife and fire.

ORESTES: Say no such thing! My own ill-luck I must accept;
When this one pain confronts me, I will not bear two.
This shame you speak of, this dishonour, lies no less
On me, if I repay your comradeship with death.
It is no hardship to me to let go a life
So persecuted by the gods. But you are rich,
Your house is pure, untainted; I am bloodguilty
And outcast. You will escape; my sister, whom I gave
To you as wife, will bear you children; so my name
Will be perpetuated, and my father's house
Will not, for want of true-born sons, be blotted out.
Go, then, and live, and take up your inheritance.

    And when you come to Hellas, when you see again
The chariots of Argos, then do this for me,
Which I solemnly lay upon you: build a tomb,
And on the mound set a memorial of me,
And let my sister come to weep and dedicate
Her lock of hair. Tell her I perished purified
For sacrifice before an altar, at the hands
Of an Argive woman. And, dear friend, never desert
My sister, when you see her family extinct
And her house desolate. Good-bye, then; you and I
Have hunted together, and grown up together; you
Have shouldered many burdens of my wretched life;
And you have been to me the dearest of my friends.

    For myself – I am the dupe of Apollo's oracles.
He built on my compliance with his earlier bidding
To drive me out of Hellas to the ends of the earth.
I placed my whole life in his hands, obeyed his word,
And killed my mother; now it is my turn to die.

PYLADES: I will raise your tomb, Orestes, and will not desert
    Your sister; for you will be an even dearer friend
    Dying than living. But the god's oracle has not
    Destroyed you yet, however close you are to death.
    Sometimes, somehow, extraordinary misfortune seems
    To take, by pure chance, some extraordinary turn.

ORESTES: No more. Phoebus' pronouncements are no help to
    me.
    Look now – here comes the priestess from the temple door.
                Enter IPHIGENIA.

IPHIGENIA: Guards, now go into the temple and make every-
    thing
    Ready for those who are to perform the sacrifice.
    [*To* ORESTES *and* PYLADES] Here is my letter, friends,
    written on several folds.
    Attend now to what further I require. A man
    In difficulties is not the same man when fear fades
    And confidence returns. The one who means to take
    This letter to Argos may, once safely away from shore,
    Neglect the task I have laid on him. This is my fear.

ORESTES: What do you desire, then? What thought makes you
    hesitate?

IPHIGENIA: Let him swear to me that he will convey this
    letter
    To Argos, and deliver it to those friends I name.

ORESTES: And in return will you swear a like oath to him?

IPHIGENIA: Tell me what I should swear to do or not to do.

ORESTES: To send him out of this territory alive and safe.

IPHIGENIA: Of course; how could he take my message other-
    wise?

ORESTES: But will the Taurian king consent to such a promise?

IPHIGENIA: I will persuade him; and will myself see Pylades
    On board.

ORESTES [*to* PYLADES]: Swear, then. [*To* IPHIGENIA]
    Prescribe for him a pious oath.

IPHIGENIA: Say this: I will deliver this letter to your friends.

PYLADES: I will indeed deliver this letter to your friends.

IPHIGENIA: And I will send you safely beyond the Purple
Rocks.

PYLADES: And what god do you invoke as witness to this
promise?

IPHIGENIA: I invoke Artemis, in whose temple I am priestess.

PYLADES: And I invoke the lord of heaven, almighty Zeus.

IPHIGENIA: And if you should neglect your oath and wrong
my trust?

PYLADES: May I not see home again! And if you fail to save
My life?

IPHIGENIA: May I not live to stand on Argive soil!

PYLADES: Listen: there is one further point we have omitted.

IPHIGENIA: If it is fair, there is still time to speak of it.

PYLADES: Allow me this provision: should my ship be
wrecked,
My goods lost, and your letter with them, and I escape
With my skin only, then this oath shall not be binding.

IPHIGENIA: You know what?24 I will take steps to make
doubly sure.
I will say over to you now the words written
In the letter; then you can repeat them to my friends.
In this way safety is assured: if you preserve
The letter, then the written words themselves will speak
Their silent message; if the letter's lost at sea,
But you are safe, then my words will be safe with you.

PYLADES: Agreed; that will best serve both your concern and
mine.
Tell me the man to whom I must deliver this
In Argos, and the message I'm to learn by heart.

IPHIGENIA: Say this to Orestes, Agamemnon's son: 'This
message
Is sent by Iphigenia, who was sacrificed
At Aulis. She is alive, though dead to all her friends.'

ORESTES: Alive? Where is she? Has she come back from the dead?

IPHIGENIA: I am here, before your eyes. But wait – you interrupt.

'My brother, bring me home, before I die, to Argos
Out of this savage country, and release me from
My priesthood in this temple of Artemis, where I
Preside over the ritual death of travellers – '

ORESTES: Pylades, what is this? Where are we? In a dream?

IPHIGENIA: ' – Or I shall haunt your house, Orestes, with a curse' –

I say his name once more, that you may learn it well.

PYLADES: Ye gods!

IPHIGENIA: Why call the gods? What is my brother to you?

PYLADES: Nothing – continue; my thought strayed to other matters.

[*Aside*] If I ask no questions, maybe I shall hear the truth.

IPHIGENIA: Tell him that Artemis saved me from my father's hands;

That the sharp sword, with which he thought he struck me, fell
Instead on a deer, which she provided in my place;
That she then brought me to live here. This is your charge;
That is the written message which this tablet holds.

PYLADES: Oh, lady! You have bound me with an easy oath,
In exchange for a fair promise. I will lose no time
In making good the oath I swore. Orestes, look!
From your own sister I deliver you this letter.

ORESTES: I accept it. But, to embrace this joy, what do I want
With folded tablets, written words? Away with them!
– My dearest sister! I am so wild with wonderment
At what I have heard, I hardly can believe it true.
Yet welcome happiness! Let me take you in my arms!

CHORUS: Stop, stranger! Take away your hands! They dese-
crate
The holy robes of Artemis' priestess. You do wrong.

ORESTES: My own sister! We have one father — you and I
Are both Agamemnon's children; don't turn from me now!
You have your brother, whom you never hoped to see.

IPHIGENIA: What? You my brother? Come, no more of this.
My brother
Is well enough known in Argos, and in Nauplia too.

ORESTES: My poor sister, your brother is not in Argos now!

IPHIGENIA: But — Clytemnestra of Sparta was your mother,
then?

ORESTES: Yes, by my father, Pelops' grandson, Agamemnon.

IPHIGENIA: What are you saying? Have you some evidence of
this?

ORESTES: I have. Just question me about our family. 25

IPHIGENIA: Better, surely, for you to speak, and I will listen.

ORESTES: I will speak first of things Electra told me — this:
You know that Atreus and Thyestes nursed a feud?

IPHIGENIA: I heard of it; they quarrelled over a golden lamb.

ORESTES: So, you recall weaving this story on your loom?

IPHIGENIA: You touch my heart there, dear one — I almost
believe.

ORESTES: Also in your fine tapestry — the sun turned back!

IPHIGENIA: This picture too I delicately wove.

ORESTES: Your mother
Sent holy water to Aulis for your wedding-day.

IPHIGENIA: I know; that was because I was to marry a prince.

ORESTES: Yes, and you sent your mother a lock of your own
hair.

IPHIGENIA: True — for a burial-token in my body's place.

ORESTES: And now a proof I have seen with my own eyes —
hidden
In your room in our father's palace — that old spear
Which Pelops hurled to kill Oenomaus at Pisa

And win the virgin Hippodamia for his bride.

IPHIGENIA: You are Orestes! Oh, my dearest, dearest
   brother!
   I have found you, so far from home,
   From Argos – O my dear one!

ORESTES: And I have found you living, whom everyone
   thought dead.
   Your eyes are wet with tears – mine too; but they are tears
   Of happiness; our weeping and our joy are one.

IPHIGENIA: He was a baby when I left him –
   So young, so young in his nurse's arms at home.
   O my heart, happier than words can tell!
   What can I say? This day has come to us
   Beyond wonder, beyond thought!

ORESTES: May we together find good fortune in time to
   come!

IPHIGENIA: O friends, I hold a miracle of joy;
   I fear it will escape out of my hands
   Flying up to the sky.
   My own dear city, Mycenae,
   Altar and hearth the Cyclops built,
   Hear my heart's thanks for my brother's life,
   Thanks for your care that reared him
   A light of hope for our house!

ORESTES: Our house, our race, is noble; but the destiny
   That both our lives were born to, sister, is accursed.

IPHIGENIA: I know, to my sorrow,[26] well I know
   How my unhappy father laid the knife to my throat.

ORESTES: That fearful sight I never saw, my mind's eye sees.

IPHIGENIA: No wedding-hymn was chanted
   When treacherously they led me
   Decked as a bride for Achilles' bed,
   And the altar of joy was ringed with tears and groaning,
   And the ritual cleansing mocked with guilt.

ORESTES: I too shudder, to think my father could do that.

IPHIGENIA: Had I a father? How can I call him father?
So from one fertile crime
Fate leads us blindly to the next.

ORESTES How nearly, sister, your own hand had shed my
blood!

IPHIGENIA: What was I doing? Brother, how horrible!
How close I was to horror! How slender a chance
Saved you from death and me from bloody defilement!
And now, how will it end? Will luck be timely?
What device of mine can help you
Quit the land and cheat the altar,
Send you living back to Argos
Now, before the knife can taste your blood?
Think, my despairing brain – the way is for you to find!
By land, leaving the ship – trust to your heels?
You would die among savage tribes and trackless deserts.
No, you must fly by ship,
Make for the Blue Strait and the Narrow Rocks –
A weary, endless journey – gods have mercy!
I am helpless, helpless! O my brother,
What aid from earth or heaven,
What miracle past hoping
Could work the impossible,
And save our lives, the last remaining
Glimmers of hope for the House of Atreus?

CHORUS: This meeting is a marvel words could not describe,
Nor ears believe, had I not seen it with my own eyes.

PYLADES: Orestes, it is natural that your sister and you
Should embrace each other, meeting after so many years.
But now you must put feeling aside and concentrate
On one grand theme – to escape out of this savage place
To safety. We must not flout Fortune, or waste time
However delightfully, but seize the chance we have.

ORESTES: You are right. Our safety lies, I think, as much with
Chance

As with ourselves; yet, if we play a resolute part,
Surely the gods will be the stronger on our side.

IPHIGENIA: Let him not stop me [27] – it's no hindrance to our plans –
From asking first about Electra; any news
Of her is precious. What is happening to her life?

ORESTES: She is wife to Pylades here. All goes well with her.

IPHIGENIA: Of what city is Pylades? Who is his father?

ORESTES: He is of Phocis. Strophius is his father's name.

IPHIGENIA: Why, then, he is Atreus' grandson, and related to me.

ORESTES: Indeed, yes, he's your cousin; and my one tried friend.

IPHIGENIA: But he was not born when my father took my life.

ORESTES: True; it was some time before Strophius had a child.

IPHIGENIA: My sister's husband, Pylades – give me your hand!

ORESTES: To me he is more than cousin; I owe him my life.

IPHIGENIA: What steeled you to so dread an act as matricide?

ORESTES: Let us not speak of it. I avenged my father's death.

IPHIGENIA: But why did she kill him? What was her reason for it?

ORESTES: Don't ask about her; it is not fit for you to hear.

IPHIGENIA: I am silent. Are you now the lord, and hope, of Argos?

ORESTES: I am an exile. Menelaus rules Argos.

IPHIGENIA: What? Did our uncle choose our day of stress to turn
Traitor?

ORESTES: No. Dread of pursuing Furies banishes me.

IPHIGENIA: Here too – they told me – on the shore, the fit seized you.

ORESTES: It's not the first time men have witnessed what I suffer.

IPHIGENIA: I know: the Furies drive you for our mother's
     sake.

ORESTES: They do; under their cruel bridles I drip blood.

IPHIGENIA: What could have made you travel to this distant
     coast?

ORESTES: I came in obedience to Apollo's oracle.

IPHIGENIA: May his command be spoken of? What must you
     do?

ORESTES: I'll tell you. This is how all my sufferings began.
     When first my hands were burdened with my mother's –
       with
     Matters I will not speak of, I was hounded on
     This way and that, an exile, by the Furies; till
     At last Apollo sent me to Athens, to appear
     On trial indicted by the Nameless Goddesses.
     For in Athens sits an inviolable court
     Which Zeus established long ago to arraign Ares
     Upon some charge of murder. When I first came there,
     They all refused me shelter, as a man hated
     By gods; but some took pity on me, and let me sit
     As guest in the same room with them, at a separate
     Table; [28] and so, making me eat and drink apart,
     Barred me from converse. They would pour into each man's
       bowl
     An equal share of wine, and so enjoy their feast.
     They were my hosts – I thought it well not to protest;
     I grieved in silence, seeming oblivious of their slight,
     Lamenting loudly that I was a matricide.
     (Since then, they tell me, Athenians commemorate
     My unhappy visit by a yearly festival
     Known as the Feast of Pitchers, honoured to this day.)
        I appeared before the court that meets on Ares' Hill;
     I stood there on a dais on one side of the court,
     The eldest of the Erinyes stood opposite.
     They charged me with my mother's murder; I replied.

The votes were counted equal, and Athena raised
Her hand for my acquittal. I had stood for trial
On a capital charge, and won my case. Those Furies then
Who accepted the court's judgement fixed their permanent
Shrine near the court itself; those who rejected it
Continued still to persecute me from place to place
Until I came again to Apollo's holy ground.
I lay starving, prostrate, before his sanctuary
And swore to end my life there, unless he, who had
Destroyed me, would now save me. Then Apollo's word,
Voiced from the golden tripod, sent me to this country,
To take the statue of Artemis that fell from heaven
And set it up in Athens. Help me then to achieve
This deed which the god prescribed for my deliverance!
Once we secure this holy image, I shall be free
Of madness, we can escape with you to our well-manned
    ship,
Sail for Mycenae, and bring you to your home again.
O dearest, dearest sister, save our father's house,
And save me too. My life, and our whole family,
Must perish, unless that god-sent statue can be ours.

CHORUS: Surely some seething anger of gods has raged against
    The sons of Tantalus, dragging them through endless
    troubles.

IPHIGENIA: I longed, even before you came here, to return
    To Argos, brother, and to see you once again.
    And now my wish is matched with yours — first, to release
    You from your torments; next, renouncing bitterness
    Against the hand that offered me in sacrifice,
    To restore the shattered fortunes of my father's house.
    So my hand would be guiltless of your blood, and we
    Could all be saved. But I am afraid of Artemis,
    Whom we cannot deceive, and of the king, when he
    Finds the stone pedestal plundered of its effigy.
    What answer could excuse me? It would be certain death.

If these two ends could be accomplished at one stroke –
To steal the statue, and bring me on board your ship,
Then it's well worth the danger. If you can't do both,
If the image goes and I stay here, then I must die;
But you will achieve your object and get safely home.
If I can save you, I do not shrink even from death.
No family can afford to let its men be killed;
A woman's help is feeble in comparison.

ORESTES: My mother's blood is on my hands; that is enough –
I will not add yours. I mean to share equally
With you either in life or death. Think of this too:
If carrying off her statue to the city of Athens
Could cause offence to Artemis, would Apollo then
. Have bidden me do it? Or was this his plan, to send
Me here to re-unite us?[30] I see many threads
Drawing together; I believe we shall reach home!

IPHIGENIA: How can we do two things at once, escape dying
And steal the statue? This is where our hopes of home
Are weakest. Let's consult, then, and work out some plan.

ORESTES: Would it be possible to assassinate the king?

IPHIGENIA: No; that would violate the law of guest and host.

ORESTES: If doing it would save us, we must take the risk.

IPHIGENIA: I praise your courage; but I could not think of
it.

ORESTES: Could you hide me inside the temple? Would that
work?

IPHIGENIA: To wait till darkness comes, and then make our
escape?

ORESTES: Yes; night's the time for thieves, daylight for
honesty.

IPHIGENIA: There are the temple guards inside; we should be
caught.

ORESTES: Heaven help us, then, we're lost; what other way
is there?

IPHIGENIA: I think, now, I begin to see another way.

ORESTES: What way? What are you thinking? Come, I want to know.

IPHIGENIA: I could use your misfortune to deceive the king.

ORESTES: Let's have it, then; that's like a woman's cleverness.

IPHIGENIA: I'll say you have come from Argos with your mother's blood
Fresh on your hands.

ORESTES: Yes, use my guilt, if that will help.

IPHIGENIA: I'll tell them it would be impious to offer you
To Artemis.

ORESTES: For what reason? I begin to see.

IPHIGENIA: You are unclean; the victim offered must be pure.

ORESTES: How does that help us get the statue of Artemis?

IPHIGENIA: I shall need to purify your body in the sea.

ORESTES: But we came to get the statue, and it's still in there.

IPHIGENIA: I'll say that it too must be cleansed, that you touched it.

ORESTES: Cleansed – where? Out on the wet rocks of that headland –

IPHIGENIA: Yes,
Out there, where your ship's hempen bridles hold her fast.

ORESTES: Will you yourself carry the image, or someone else?

IPHIGENIA: I will. To touch it is permitted to me alone.

ORESTES: And Pylades – what part shall he be given in this?

IPHIGENIA: I'll tell them his hands carry the same taint as yours.

ORESTES: Will you do this with the king's knowledge or without?

IPHIGENIA: My story will convince him; he will have to know.

ORESTES: Well, my ship's crew are only waiting to dip oars.

IPHIGENIA: Indeed, that part of our plan must be left to you.

ORESTES: One other thing: these women here must keep our secret.

Beg for their help, summon your most persuasive words;
There's nothing stirs compassion like a woman's plea.
The rest I'll see to; and may Fortune smile on us!

IPHIGENIA [*to the* CHORUS]: Dear friends, it is to you I
    look; for in your hands
Rests my whole future – either to find happiness
Or to be nothing, to be for ever separated
From home, and from the brother and sister whom I love.
Let the first word of my appeal to you be this:
We are women. Women have a feeling for one another;
They share and keep a secret with unfaltering faith.
Say nothing! Help us carry out this difficult
Escape. True honour lives in a trustworthy tongue.
A single chance determines for three loving lives
Between a safe homecoming and the stroke of death.
If I live, I will come and bring you back to Hellas
To share my happy fortune. [*She addresses them one by one*]
                            I beg you, and you;
I take your hand, I touch your cheek, your knees; and you
I bid think of the dear ones in your home – parents
Or children: which of you will promise, or refuse,
To help us? Speak; what is your answer? If I fail
To win your hearts, my brother's life and mine are lost.

CHORUS: Dear mistress, have no fear; only get safely away.
I give my word: our silence shall reveal nothing –
Great Zeus be witness – of what you entrust to us.

IPHIGENIA: Heaven bless you for that promise, and bring
    you happiness!
– Brother, and Pylades, go into the temple now.
The king will be here presently, to ascertain
Whether the strangers have been duly sacrificed.
Artemis! You who once in Aulis Bay delivered
Me from my father's murderous hand, now save us all;
Or prove to all men that Apollo's word is false.
Be gracious; come with us out of this savage land

To Athens. Here is no fit place to make your home;
There a city of gladness waits to welcome you.

Exeunt into the temple.

CHORUS: Bird of the sharp sea-cliffs,   [*Strophe*
  Halcyon, chanting your mournful note —
  A cry that speaks to the understanding heart,
  A ceaseless song to your lost lover:
  I match with yours my wingless song of sorrow,
  Longing for the festivals of Hellas,
  Where the people of my country gather;
  Longing for an Artemis whose worship is joy,
  Who has her temple by the Cynthian hill
  Where soft-haired palm and shapely laurel grow,
  And the silver-green of the holy olive
  Which sheltered Leto in her labour;
  The round lake where water slowly turns,
  Where the swan's chant honours the Muses.

  O tears, falling tears   [*Antistrophe*
  That streamed over my cheeks
  When weapons crowded through the breached wall
  And enemy ships rowed us away!
  Bought for a weight of gold,
  I reached this barbarous coast,
  Where I serve Agamemnon's daughter,
  Priestess of the deer-slaying goddess,
  Attend her altars red with blood not of lambs;
  Envying their fate who have been
  Unfortunate all their life long,
  Whose hearts necessity and old grief
  Have steeled to endurance from their birth.
  Misery which follows happiness
  Crushes the mortal spirit with despair.

  And you, princess —   [*Strophe*

A fifty-oared Argive galley will bear you home;
And the whistling wax-bound pipe of Pan-of-the-mountain
Shall shrill to the rowers' rhythm;
And the prophet-singer Apollo
With the ring of his seven-stringed lyre
Shall escort you safe to the shining land of Athens;
And as your swift craft speeds on the oar-blades' foamy
    track,
As sheets and forestay strain
And the sail swells over the bows,
You will leave me here.

Oh, if I could travel that shining track　　　　[Antistrophe
Where the sun rides his chariot in fiery splendour!
I would fold impatient wings over weary shoulders
Above the room that was mine in childhood;
With yearning thoughts I remember
The weddings in noble houses, the whirl of dancing,
The bridesmaids singing together, and I among them,
In pride of youth and delicate ornament
And glory of rival graces;
When I would wear bright-coloured scarves
Which flowed with my long hair to shade my cheek!

Enter THOAS, *with guards.*

THOAS: Where is the Hellene woman, the temple-guardian?
    Has she performed the proper ceremonies? And are
    The strangers' bodies blazing in the sanctuary?
CHORUS: King, she is here herself, and will tell you every-
    thing.

Enter IPHIGENIA, *carrying the image of Artemis.*

THOAS: Why, priestess! That is the holy statue in your arms!
    Why do you move it from its inviolable place?
IPHIGENIA: King, stand there by the pillars; take no further
    step.

THOAS: But, Iphigenia, what has been happening in the temple?

IPHIGENIA: Silence! [31] May the gods guard us from impurity!

THOAS: Impurity? Tell me plainly what this mystery means.

IPHIGENIA: I found those men you caught a tainted sacrifice.

THOAS: And what revealed this to you? Or is it your surmise?

IPHIGENIA: The holy image shrank backward on its pedestal.

THOAS: Not of itself? Surely the earth shook and made it move!

IPHIGENIA: Of itself. The statue trembled, and its eyelids closed.

THOAS: What can have been the cause? These men's impurity?

IPHIGENIA: This, nothing else. They have committed fearful crimes.

THOAS: They may have killed one of my people on the shore.

IPHIGENIA: No; they came here already foul with kindred blood.

THOAS: What blood? A strange desire to learn comes over me.

IPHIGENIA: Their mother's. Their two hands on one sword took her life.

THOAS: Apollo! Even a savage would recoil from that.

IPHIGENIA: They have been hounded out of every city in Hellas.

THOAS: I see now — this is why you have brought the statue out —

IPHIGENIA: Out under the pure heaven, to be purged of blood.

THOAS: You recognized the stain on these men: tell me how.

IPHIGENIA: When the holy image turned away, I questioned them.

THOAS: Your Hellene intuition led you to the truth.

IPHIGENIA: And they held out a pleasing bait to win my heart.

THOAS: Oh? Tempted you with news from Argive friends, perhaps?

IPHIGENIA: They tell me Orestes, the only brother I have, is well.

THOAS: They hoped you'd spare them in delight at such good news.

IPHIGENIA: And that my father is alive and prospering.

THOAS: You of course ignored them, knowing your duty to Artemis.

IPHIGENIA: Hellas destroyed me; I hate Hellas utterly.

THOAS: Well, now, tell me what we should do with these two men.

IPHIGENIA: There is no choice; we shall observe the established law.

THOAS: To work, then, with your holy water and your sword!

IPHIGENIA: First I must bathe and purify their tainted flesh.

THOAS: Where, then? In fresh spring-water, or in the salt sea?

IPHIGENIA: The sea can wash clean all the foulness of mankind.

THOAS: Their sacrifice will be the more acceptable.

IPHIGENIA: My part in this will also be the better done.

THOAS: Well, here at hand, close by the temple, the surf breaks.

IPHIGENIA: Solitude is needful; there will be certain other rites.

THOAS: Go where you wish; I'll not pry into mysteries.

IPHIGENIA: I must purify too the statue of Artemis.

THOAS: If it is tainted with the guilt of matricide –

IPHIGENIA: If not, I would never have moved it from its pedestal.

THOAS: Of course. Your care and piety are very proper.

IPHIGENIA: Listen now to what I shall require.

THOAS: It is for you to say.

IPHIGENIA: First, then, bind the strangers' arms with cords.

THOAS: Why, where could they escape?

IPHIGENIA: Never trust a man from Hellas.

THOAS: Guards, get ropes and tie them up.

IPHIGENIA: Let your servants bring the men out here before
the temple, and
Wrap their cloaks over their heads –

THOAS: In reverence for the sun's pure light.

IPHIGENIA: Send some of your soldiers with me,

THOAS: These men shall accompany you.

IPHIGENIA: Send a herald through the city telling all the
citizens
To remain inside their houses –

THOAS: To avoid all contact with
Guilty blood?

IPHIGENIA: Yes, all pollution must be shunned.

THOAS [to a guard]:   Go, command this.

IPHIGENIA: No one must set eyes on them.

THOAS: You are thoughtful for my citizens.

IPHIGENIA: For my friends too – those who have a special
claim.

THOAS: You think of me.

IPHIGENIA: Naturally.

THOAS: And it is natural that our city honours you.
What more must I do?

IPHIGENIA: Stay here and purify with fire the whole
Sanctuary for Artemis.

THOAS: It shall be clean when you return.

IPHIGENIA: When the men come from the temple, hold your
cloak before your eyes.

THOAS: This will guard me from defilement.

IPHIGENIA: If I seem to stay too long –

THOAS: Well, how soon should I expect you?

IPHIGENIA: There's no need to feel disturbed.

THOAS: Take what time is needful to perform the rites with
proper care.

IPHIGENIA: God grant that this cleansing prosper as I wish!

THOAS: God grant it so!

The temple doors open, and ORESTES *and* PYLADES *come forward bound, with cloaks over their heads, led by guards and temple-attendants.*

IPHIGENIA: Now I see the two men coming from the temple; at their side

Servants bear the sacred robes, and two young lambs, with whose pure blood

I will purge the taint of murder, burning lamps, and other choice

Emblems which I have prescribed to cleanse the image and these men.

She raises the image, and the procession forms.

I warn every citizen; keep far from the unholy thing,

Every temple-ministrant whose hands are sacred to the gods,

All who go today to join their hands in marriage, every womb

Heavy with child: away! Depart, lest this defilement fall on you!

Virgin child of Zeus and Leto, Artemis! If I may purge

These men's guilt, if we may sacrifice where sacrifice is right,

Your shrine shall be clean, and we shall prosper well. The rest I pray

Without words, to gods who know all things, [32] and, Artemis, to you.

IPHIGENIA, ORESTES, PYLADES *and several guards go out towards the shore in solemn procession.* THOAS *and the remaining guards go into the temple.*

CHORUS: Long ago in Delos, in a valley of fruit-   *[Strophe*
       trees,

Leto gave birth to a lovely son and daughter:

Apollo the golden-haired, skilful on the lyre,

And Artemis, queen of the well-aimed bow.
Then from the sea-girt ridge,
From the spot famed for their birth, she brought them
To Mount Parnassus, mother of surging streams,
Whose slopes ring with revels of Dionysus.
There the dragon with wine-red eyes,
With body of bronze and coloured scales,
As fierce a monster as land or sea can show,
Lay in the leafy laurel-shade
Guarding the ancient oracle of the Earth.
Though you were still, Phoebus, a little child,
Still dancing in your mother's arms,
Yet you killed the dragon, and became
Successor to the sacred oracle.
Seated now on the golden tripod,
Throne of infallible prophecy,
Neighbour to the Castalian stream,
You send forth from your inmost sanctuary
The word of heaven to mortal men,
Lord of the central temple of all the earth.

Now when Apollo came and drove   [*Antistrophe*
Themis daughter of Earth from the holy seat of Pytho,
Earth brought forth from her womb
Shapes of dreams that appear by night; and these
Flew to the sleeping cities of men
When darkness laid them to rest,
And told them of things past and things to come.
Thus Earth, indignant for her daughter,
Stole from Apollo his temple's pride of place.
And Apollo leapt up and ran to Zeus on Olympus,
Gripped the throne with his baby hand,
Demanding rescue for the Pythian temple
From the anger of the goddess Earth.
And Zeus laughed to see how promptly the child

Presented his claim on the gold that flows from mortal
   worship.
His locks shook as he bowed assent,
Ending the utterances of dreams.
He took from men the truth of nightly visions,
Restored to Loxias his prerogative
To answer those who throng his throne from far and wide,
Chanting to the mortal race the certainties of heaven.[33]
   Enter a MESSENGER. *He ignores the* CHORUS *and*
   goes straight to the temple doors.

MESSENGER: Keepers of the temple! Officers of the altar!
   Where
   Is Thoas? Where's the king? Open these rivetted doors
   And call King Thoas to leave the temple and come out here.

CHORUS: If I may presume to speak unbidden – what is the
   matter?

MESSENGER: Those two young men have fled the country.
   Iphigenia
   Plotted the whole thing; now they've gone, and taken with
   them
   The sacred image – it lies in the hold of a Greek ship.

CHORUS: An incredible story! But if you want to see the king,
   He's not here; he has just left the temple hurriedly.

MESSENGER: Where was he going? I must inform him what
   has happened.

CHORUS: None of us knows; you had better go and search for
   him;
   You will soon find him and be able to give your news.

MESSENGER: Hear that! I never trust a word a woman says.
   You're in this plot with all the rest – I'm sure of it.

CHORUS: You're mad; what could we have to do with the
   men's escape?
   Be off to your master's palace as fast as possible.

MESSENGER: Not till I know for certain what I want to
   know [34] –

Whether the king's inside the temple or not. — Ho, there!
Unbolt the doors, you in the temple! Tell the king
I'm here outside, to bring him a packet of bad news.

He hammers at the temple door, till it opens
and Thoas comes out, attended.

THOAS: Who makes this outcry at the porch of Artemis,
  Hammering the door till the whole shrine reverberates?

MESSENGER: What's this? These women were trying to send
  me off again —
  Told me you had gone; and you were inside all the time!

THOAS: What did they hope to gain by that? What are they
  after?

MESSENGER: I'll speak of them another time. Now listen to
  More urgent matters. Iphigenia, who presides
  Over these altars, has escaped with the young men —
  Fled the country, and taken with her the holy image
  Of Artemis. That purification was a trick.

THOAS: The priestess — gone? What ill-wind makes that possible?

MESSENGER: This will surprise you more: it was to save
  Orestes!

THOAS: Orestes? No! You don't mean Clytemnestra's son?

MESSENGER: I do; the victim consecrated to Artemis.

THOAS: It's a miracle; or should I use a stronger word?

MESSENGER: Don't turn your mind to all that now, but
  listen to me;
  And when the facts are clear before you, then think out
  What's the best way to hunt and catch these foreigners.

THOAS: You're quite right; tell me everything. They have a
  long
  Hard voyage before them, if they hope to escape my sword.

MESSENGER: When we had reached the edge of the sea, not
  far from where
  Orestes' ship was waiting, anchored out of sight,

Iphigenia silently motioned to us guards,
Whom you had sent holding the men, to stand apart
While she kindled the holy flame and carried out
The rites of purification. They walked on alone,
The men in front and she behind holding the cord
That bound them. This made us uneasy; but, my lord,
Your servants thought all was in order. Presently,
To make us think she was busy with the ceremony,
She gave a piercing cry, and then began to intone
Wild magical incantations, as if actually
Washing off blood. Well, we sat there, and time went on;
Until we thought perhaps the men had broken loose,
Killed her, and run for it; but we sat on, fearing
To see what was forbidden. But at last we all
Agreed, in spite of orders, to go and join the rest.

We went; and there we saw the hull of a Greek ship,
Her oars, in two lines, lifted like a pair of wings,
And fifty rowers at the ready; [35] the two men,
Freed from their bonds, were on shore, standing near the
   stern.
Some of the crew were steadying the prow with poles,
Some lashing the anchors to the bulwarks, others again
Letting down ladders for the two men to climb aboard. [36]

So, when we saw this treachery, without more scruple
We ran and held Iphigenia, seized the cables,
And tried to unship the steering-oars; and we were shouting,
'Who and what are you? And what right have you to come
Stealing our images and temple-officers,
Smuggling this woman out of the country?' And he said,
'My name's Orestes, let me tell you; I'm her brother,
And now I'm going to take my long-lost sister home.'

We still held fast to Iphigenia, and did our best
To drag her away to you, sir; but we paid for it
In hard knocks and bruised faces, as you see. Those two
Had no swords, nor we either; but they came at us

With fists and feet; and both of them, this side and that,
Aimed at us such a volley of blows, that to resist
Was to reel back wounded and dazed. They stamped their
    seal
On every man; and we retired, with heads broken
And bleeding eyes, to a spur of rock. There we stood firm
And fought with greater caution, hurling stones at them.
But we were soon stopped; archers came up on the poop
And drove us back with a hail of arrows. At that moment
A wave lifted the ship a little inshore; the foam
Swirled at Iphigenia's feet – she shrank away;
Orestes hoisted her on his left shoulder, strode
Into the sea, leapt at the ladder, and set down
His sister safely inside the ship, together with
The holy statue of Artemis which fell from heaven.

At once from the ship's centre rose a ringing voice:
'Seamen of Hellas, grip your oars; churn the waves white!
For this we sailed through the Symplegades into
The Sullen Sea; and we have what we came to get!'

The crew replied with a triumphant roar. The oars
Plunged, and the ship went gliding through the harbour
    mouth –
While still in sheltered water. Once outside, she met
A choppy swell, and going was hard. A sudden wind
Blew strongly, and forced the ship back stern foremost. The
    men
Struggled, kicking against the current; still the ship
Was driven backward towards the land. Then Iphigenia
Stood up and prayed: 'I am your priestess, Artemis;
Bring me safe home to Hellas from this savage land!
Forgive me for my theft. You, goddess, love your own
Brother; believe that I too love my nearest kin!'
Her prayer was echoed by the seamen's loud paean
To Apollo, as their bare arms tugged the straining oars
In perfect rhythm. The ship came closer, closer toward

The rocks. One of their men [37] jumped into the sea, another
Was trying to fasten a looped rope to hold the ship.
I left them and came straight here to find you, my lord,
And tell you what has been happening. So get cords, fetters,
And come at once! Unless the on-shore swell dies down
They've no hope of escape. Divine Poseidon, lord
Of the sea, is Troy's protector, and an enemy
To the house of Pelops; now, it seems, he's going to hand
Orestes over to you and to our citizens —
His sister too, who has forgotten how Artemis
Saved her at Aulis, and is guilty of treachery. [38]

CHORUS: Unhappy Iphigenia! [39] You and your brother now
Will fall again into our master's hands, and perish.

THOAS: Harness your horses, every man in my city!
After them! Ride at full speed to the shore and catch
These foreign Greeks when their ship grounds. Hunt the
    men down
With the help of divine Artemis, whom they have mocked.
Launch all our fast boats; sea or land — we'll capture them.
Then let us fling them down the rocky cliffs, impale
Their bodies on stakes! — You women, you were in this plot;
You I shall punish later, when I am at leisure;
I can't stop now, I have more important things to do.
            Several guards make off towards the shore.
            Enter, above the temple porch, ATHENA.

ATHENA: Wait, wait, King Thoas! What is this new hunt?
    How far
Will your rage take you? Hear my words; I am Athena.
Call back those armed men you sent streaming in pursuit.
        THOAS *signs to a guard, who runs.* THOAS *kneels.*
It was the word of Destiny, from Apollo's mouth,
That sent Orestes, flying before the Furies' wrath,
Here to this shore, to bring his sister home to Argos,
Convey the holy image to my Attic soil,
And win release from the anguish that now haunts his life.

That is my word to you. As for Poseidon, he
Does not, as you suppose, purpose Orestes' death
In the engulfing waves, but has, at my request, 40
Already calmed their uproar, and has bidden the sea
Provide a smooth path for Orestes' homeward voyage.

And you, Orestes – for an immortal's voice reaches
Your ears, though far off – hear now my commands: sail on
With the holy emblem and your sister; and when you reach
The god-built city of Athens, there is a holy place
Called by my people Halae, near the very edge
Of Attic soil, neighbour to the Carystian Rock;
There you shall build a shrine, and set the image therein.
Name it the Taurian temple, to recall this land,
And all the pains you suffered, driven from end to end
Of Hellas by tormenting Furies; there shall men
Henceforth raise solemn hymns to Taurian Artemis.

Give them this law: when my people hold festival
The priest shall with his sword touch a man's throat, and
    draw
One drop of blood, as ransom for your blood now spared,
To accord due reverence and awe to Artemis.
You, Iphigenia, shall hold her sacred keys, and serve
Her shrine at the Brauronian Steps. There, when you die,
They shall adorn your grave with gowns of softest weave
Left in their store by women who die in childbed. – Thoas,
These women here you must send home to Hellas; this
Is my command . . .41 Orestes, when you stood for trial
In Athens, and the votes were even, I gave judgement
For mercy, and you live. Let this be law for ever:
When equal votes are counted, you shall spare the accused
And not condemn. So, son of Agamemnon, take
Your sister home; and Thoas, you must be content.
THOAS: Divine Athena, to receive a god's command
    And disobey, is madness; therefore I renounce
    All anger against Orestes for the holy image

He has taken from me, and bear his sister no ill-will.
No honour comes of matching strength with mighty gods.
Let them go safely with the image to your land
And there set up a home for Artemis. Moreover,
I will send home to Hellas and to happiness
These women, as your word commands me. The armed
    force,
The ships of war, I sent against the foreigners,
Since you, goddess, desire it, I cancel and recall.

ATHENA: You are wise. The gods themselves bow to Necessity,
    Not only you. Blow, winds, and bear Orestes on
    To Athens! I will go with them, to keep watch over
    The holy statue of my sister Artemis.

                    Exit ATHENA.

CHORUS: Go, and good go with you,
    Rich in Fortune's favour,
    Numbered with the living!
    Great Athena, honoured by immortal gods,
    Held in awe by mortal men,
    We will do what you command.
    Past all wonder, now to our despairing ears
    Lips divine have spoken
    Words of joy and comfort! 42

NOTES FOR ALCESTIS

1. *mourning*: literally, 'the thud of hands', i.e., on the head or breast.

2. *I alone*: I have adopted here a slight deviation from the MSS, suggested by Murray in the *app. crit.* of his Oxford Text.

3. *not to desert him*: the verb here is the same as that translated in line 180 as 'be false to'. The irony is intense: Admetus is saying to Alcestis both 'Don't die for me' and 'Die for me'. His whole dilemma is contained in this one word, as the next sentence, 'He asks the impossible', points out.

4. *not worth living*: the Chorus agree with the Servant (line 198) that the implications of marriage put an honourable man in an impossible position. When Admetus 'has suffered' (line 145) he will make the same discovery, lines 935–61.

5. *He is a good man*: Literally, 'since he is not deficient in understanding'. Greek words which refer primarily to the intellect frequently carry a moral reference as well.

6. *reverse your passage*: Literally, to bring you back 'with riverwise and nether oar'. It is hard to ascribe any poetic value to this line. Equally it is rash, when considering the line in relation to lines 252ff., 361, 439–41, 444, simply to remark that the poet was falling below his usual standard of competence. The precision and thoroughness with which the vocabulary of the whole play is designed (see Introduction, p. 15. and the two articles referred to in footnotes) make this an improbable explanation. Rather I would suspect irony here. At the heart of the play lies a serious presentation of the sternness of Necessity and the fact of death; and this is the theme of the third stasimon, 962–1005. Here in the first stasimon the chorus use the popular imagery of death and the lower world; and this, though it shapes the imagination of Alcestis herself (252ff.) and of Admetus (258, 900–902), is in fact stripped of validity by the tiresome repetitions of the chorus in this stasimon. (So Heracles, 493–5, mocks the credulity of the Pheraean Elders.) The entry of death into a living household is treated in this play with a realism which makes the fairytale of Charon and his row-boat seem childish and irrelevant; and of

this, the semi-comic banality of the chorus's conventional terms conveys a warning. To represent this in a translation, however, is almost impossible.

7. At this point a line is missing in the MSS.

8. *I shall still be deeply in your debt*: Heracles means, 'I shall be grateful for hospitality offered, even if I decline it.' But the phrase also carries, for the audience, an allusion to that debt which Heracles, by accepting hospitality, will soon discover, acknowledge, and discharge.

9. *to burial*: the Greek says, 'to burial and pyre'; and throughout the play Euripides seems to invest the disposal of the corpse with intentional vagueness.

10. Four lines follow here which may have been interpolated, and are omitted by some editors. Their sense is: 'Nor is she my mother who claims to be and is so called; but I was born from a slave, and secretly given to your wife to nurse.'

11. *our one life*: a difficult line to translate, because the English word 'life' means both 'a span of life' and 'a living person'. An alternative rendering is 'Each of us has to answer for one life, not two.'

12. *in her grave*: literally, 'on the pyre'. See note 9.

13. *dost thou understand . . . ?* In order to sound impressive Heracles uses an archaic verb-form here; but he does not keep it up.

14. *say . . . day . . . way . . .*: this represents four rhymed line-endings in the Greek – an alcoholic inadvertence on Heracles' part.

15. *The cure . . .*: the Greek metaphor is of a ship *changing its anchorage*.

16. *O ravaged house!* In this *kommos* ('lament') Admetus speaks four stanzas. The first and second are followed each by an antiphonal passage shared with the chorus; the third and fourth by an admonitory comment which the chorus-leader addresses to Admetus. In the first and third of his stanzas Admetus envies the dead – thus revoking the request he had once made to his friends to die for him; in the second and fourth he envies the unmarried and childless, and recalls his wedding-day and his hopes now cut off. These lyric statements appear to be a summing-up of the immature phase of Admetus' life, from which he is about to emerge; the phase in which he could not face Necessity in the form of unexpected death, and therefore, having evaded death, devalues both life and its best gifts.

17. *I despair*: this and the next three lines given to Admetus are in Greek four different exclamations of sorrow — the kind of words of which 'alas' is almost the only English example, but which Greek possesses in abundance.

18. *sleep in her bed*? These apparently perverse suggestions are not mere empty rhetoric. In the first place they have some reason as being possible measures to secure the girl from being molested; but, more important than that, they vividly convey the fact that Admetus is mesmerized by sight of the veiled figure, whose presence exerts on him an inexplicable and irresistible attraction. His words express with psychological realism his spontaneous secret thoughts; that they are spoken aloud is timeless theatrical convention.

19. *show perfect piety*: the meaning is, that Admetus showed piety in receiving Heracles, but not in deceiving him. *As an honourable man* means 'since you wish to discharge your debt to me'. The obscurity of phrase is deliberate, and conveys the tactfulness of Heracles, who leaves his friend to work out the message for himself.

20. *flame*: the Greek word refers not to flame but to the steamy smoke which rises from burning fat.

NOTES FOR HIPPOLYTUS

[There are frequent references in these notes to Barrett's edition, Oxford, 1964]

1. *the Cyprian*: the Greek name 'Aphrodite' is native to Homeric verse and fits awkwardly into iambics; so that 'Kupris', 'the Cyprian', is almost everywhere used in tragedy. (This name, in fact, frequently drops its personal meaning and becomes an abstract noun for 'sexual love'.) In the translation I have mostly used 'Aphrodite' for the sake of clarity.

2. *the Euxine*: the Black Sea. The meaning of the word, 'friendly to strangers', is probably ironic.

3. *the Amazon*: the queen of the Amazons, Hippolyta, captured in war by Theseus. Shakespeare in *A Midsummer Night's Dream* makes her Theseus' honoured bride; but in the original legend she was a virgin queen subdued by force to the bed of her conqueror. Euripides plainly has the latter situation in mind as the psychological background of Hippolytus' character.

4. *a terrible love*: a translator has to decide whether *erōs* in any particular context is better, or less falsely, rendered by 'love' or by 'lust' – with 'passion' and 'desire' as other possibilities. In his first version of *Hippolytus* (433 B.C.) Euripides seems to have presented Phaedra's passion as 'lust'; the marked difference of treatment which we find in the surviving version (428 B.C.) may be taken to justify the use of 'love' at least in some passages. There is no reason for supposing that the poet himself held the cynical view which he gave to Hecabe in *The Women of Troy* 988–90.

5. *it bears*: the Greek verb is probably a future tense, and refers to a temple known to the audience as 'Aphrodite near Hippolytus', i.e., near his tomb.

6. *only gods must be called lord*: the dialogue between the Servant and Hippolytus is puzzling at first. Its difficulty represents the difficulty felt by the Servant in speaking unwelcome truth to his master. Hippolytus in the two minutes he has been on stage has shown that he neglects the most important of all rules – to 'think like a mortal', *thnēta phronein*. He associates with a particular goddess, and stigma-

tizes the vast majority of his fellow-humans, who worship Aphrodite, as 'impure'. The word *semnos* applied to mortals means 'proud', 'haughty'; applied to gods it means 'holy', 'great'. The Servant's somewhat devious remarks are an appeal to Hippolytus to see that he is taking on himself an attitude suitable only for gods.

7. *she has kept her body pure*: see Barrett's note on 135–8: 'the practice of fasting as an ingredient in ritual purity . . .' is 'very rare in Greek religion, but found in certain cults of Demeter . . .'.

8. *Dictynna*: a Cretan goddess, sometimes identified with Artemis. (*Dictys* is 'a hunting-net'.)

9. *along the sand-bar . . .*: See Barrett, p. 190, 383.

10. *And after this life . . .*: there is some reason for doubting the genuineness of these seven lines.

11. *A friend kills me*: the Greek word *philos* can mean not only someone who is 'dear' but someone who is 'near', i.e., a member of the same family; so the Nurse at once thinks of Theseus.

12. *My mother . . . my sister*: Pasiphaë and Ariadne. Barrett points out (p. 223) that Euripides here alludes to the earlier version of the story of Ariadne, in which she was first Dionysus' lover, and forsook the god to go with Theseus. Only this form of the story makes sense of the parallel.

13. Lines 385–7 are a famous puzzle. It is possible that, as some editors believe, they are an interpolation. Barrett accepts them as genuine and expounds them convincingly pp. 230–31; but since, even with his exposition, they remain very hard to translate, I omit them from the text of the play and give an approximate rendering here as follows:

> . . . many pleasures –
> Long hours of talking; idleness, a pleasing plague;
> And modest deference – this is of two kinds: the one
> May be a virtue, the other will destroy a house.
> If we could be sure which kind was appropriate,
> There would not be two kinds spelt with the same letters.

14. *You are beside the door*: the chorus-leader declines to leave the orchestra and join Phaedra up-stage. Nervous caution is characteristic of this chorus, as becomes clear in 785.

15. *Hippolytus*: while love was her sole emotion Phaedra could not speak his name; now that love is outweighed by desperation and anger,

she can. Note also that in this dialogue she is calm, speaking in iambics; while the chorus, in lyric metre, are excited.

16. *from today's wreck*: Barrett's accurate version of this line is: 'and myself gain what will advantage me now things have fallen out as they have'. This, and the familiarity of nautical metaphor in Greek tragedy, may excuse the introduction of an image which is not in the Greek.

17. *and learn that chastity* . . .: the Greek says simply, 'and learn to be *sōphrōn*'. *Sōphrōn* means 'of a sound mind', and refers not only to bodily chastity but to modesty and forbearance in social behaviour, and to humility before the gods. Hippolytus knows how to be 'chaste', but has yet to learn other aspects of a 'sound mind'.

18. *And left me* . . . *despair*: this is a paraphrase of a line which literally means, 'Alas, alas, these pitiful, pitiful sufferings'.

19. *with other young noblemen*: these are not the huntsmen who accompanied Hippolytus in the prologue, and who are now on the shore attending to his horses (see 1173–9). They are the friends referred to by Hippolytus in 1018 and by the Messenger in 1179–80.

20. *those rocks*: Barrett (p. 384–4) gives an account of the terrain, with a map, and mentions that the Scironian rocks are visible from the shore near Trozen, but the Isthmus itself is not; so that Euripides is using the name in a loose sense.

21. *None; since to feel* . . .: in the MSS this sentence is corrupt; but the sense given here is consonant with the tactless attitude which Hippolytus assumes towards Theseus.

22. *with the tense drumming of hooves*: literally, 'with the foot of a racing-horse'. The English version gives in words what the Greek gives by *onomatopoea*.

23. *Feet firmly in the footstalls*: see Barrett *ad loc*. The word usually means 'hunting-boots'; but here it appears to mean some kind of fitting on the chariot-floor which enabled the driver to stand firm at speed over rough ground.

24. *This sorrow* . . . *greater grief*: the obscurity of these last lines seems to cast some doubt on their genuineness. See Barrett, p. 420, where he questions whether Euripides would have referred to Hippolytus as 'great'.

NOTES FOR IPHIGENIA IN TAURIS

1. *Euripus*: the long narrow strait between the island of Euboea and the Greek mainland.

2. *fearful storms . . .*: the MSS here are confused. It is possible that line 15 refers not to storms but to a calm. The best known dramatic form of this story, in Aeschylus' *Agamemnon*, tells of a violent north-east wind; but Euripides in *Iphigenia in Aulis* (seven years after this play) clearly indicates a calm. There, however, he had special reasons for this; here it seems more likely that he kept to the familiar form of the story.

3. *Calchas*: a priest and seer who accompanied the Greek army to Troy, and who on more than one occasion declared that human sacrifice was required.

4. *Once, long ago*: these three words are not in the Greek. The style of this prologue, which tells a story familiar to most of the audience, is extremely compressed.

5. *by a custom . . .*: this line and the following are held by some to be interpolated.

6. *O Phoebus*: Orestes had been brought up near Delphi and under the influence of the Delphic priests. His murder of Clytemnestra, commanded by the oracle, was regarded by Aeschylus as just and inevitable, though disastrous. Euripides in this play seems to avoid specific condemnation; but in *Electra* (produced probably the year before) and in *Orestes* (408) the murder is treated as an outrageous crime.

7. *the Unfriendly Sea*: the Greek name for the Black Sea was *Euxeinos*, 'hospitable' – an apprehensive and propitiatory euphemism. The word *axeinos*, 'unfriendly', is itself often applied to the 'Euxine' Sea, e.g., near the opening of the first choral ode.

Euripides' geography in this play is vague and inconsistent; he sometimes makes a character speak as if the distance from Crimea to Bosphorus were only a few miles, e.g., line 746.

8. *Artemis*: the name in Greek here is 'Dictynna', a Cretan goddess of virginity and hunting, often identified with Artemis. See *Hippolytus* 145ff., note 8.

9. *Eurotas*: the river of Sparta.

10. *that first wickedness*: in the next ten lines the M SS are considerably corrupt. The 'golden lamb' referred to caused the quarrel between Atreus and Thyestes, which culminated in the 'banquet of Thyestes', at which Thyestes unwittingly ate the flesh of his own children served up to him by Atreus.

11. *Leda's daughter*: Clytemnestra was the sister of Helen.

12. *Symplegades*: the 'Clashing' Rocks, at the entrance to the Black Sea from the Bosphorus.

13. *You used to pray . . .*: See Introduction, p. 29; and lines 258–9.

14. *Dirce*: one of the two rivers of Thebes.

15. *south wind, west wind*: the geography here is more exact. The island of Leuke ('white') opposite the mouth of the Danube, and the sandbank known as 'Achilles' Course', north-west of the Taurian peninsula, would both be passed on the voyage from Bosphorus.

16. *An offering . . . abhorrent*: the chorus here illustrate the common mentality of those who at one moment boast of their country's civilized principles, and at another contradict them to gratify their own personal resentments. Since in lines 438–46 they prayed for the satisfaction of seeing Helen's throat cut, the only rational interpretation of 462–6 is as the poet's unobtrusive ironic comment on human self-delusion. See Introduction, p. 36.

17. *And Helen . . .*: Iphigenia knows, as she explained at length in 359–71, that her fate was due to her father's weakness and treachery; yet here, as there (354–8), she directs her hatred against Helen. Similarly Orestes knows that his fate is due to his murder of his mother, committed at Apollo's command; yet his desire for self-justification turns to a venomous hatred of Helen. This passage, 521–6, like similar passages in *Andromache, Hecabe, Electra*, and *Iphigenia in Aulis*, is irrelevant, irrational, and discreditable to the speakers. It seems reasonable to assume that Euripides was consciously making his comment on the readiness of men and women to ignore real causes and unite in vilifying a universal scapegoat.

18. *for him . . . who died*: the M SS reading is uncertain. The original may have been 'him who killed', in which case Iphigenia is thinking of the sacrifice at Aulis.

19. *they mean nothing*: this conclusion is even more irrational than

her interpretation of the dream in 56; for it is a long time since the strangers left Hellas. Both these irrationalities are part of Iphigenia's character, and of the drama – since meeting the Greek strangers she has lost her despondency.

20. *And what of us?*: It is unusual for a chorus to appeal so directly for a share of sympathy. The point of these lines is seen at 1056ff.; there Iphigenia needs the help of the chorus, and appeals to them with individual endearments, to which the chorus respond with a promise, later implemented at great risk to themselves. At 1420–21 the chorus think only of Iphigenia's peril, not of their own. (See Introduction, pp. 33–4.) A few lines later Iphigenia's words, 'when the same plan pleases everyone', ignore not only the chorus but Pylades, who is to die. Iphigenia's behaviour is presented as unheroic, however cogent her excuse.

21. *A letter . . . wrote for me*: this curious assumption that neither Iphigenia nor any of her Greek attendants could write has never been explained. If Phaedra could write, why not Iphigenia?

22. *no enemy to me*: some MSS, by the change of one letter, give instead the meaning 'of noble family'.

23. *will run his friend's neck into the noose*: literally, 'casts his friends' fortunes down into disasters'.

24. *You know what?* This colloquialism literally translates an idiomatic phrase common in Greek drama.

25. *question me*: the 'tokens for identification' which follow are a regular part of the story; they appear, in different ways, in Aeschylus' *Choephori* and Euripides' *Electra*.

26. *I know, to my sorrow*: see Introduction, p. 31.

27. *Let him not stop me*: this diversion has been ridiculed; but in fact, as it turns out, it leads Orestes to tell of his mission to steal the image of Artemis, and without that sequence the plot could not go forward. But there seems to be a further purpose: this ensuing dialogue directs attention yet again to the miasma of guilt, hatred, and revenge which clings to the whole family; and in particular it clarifies the outrageous nature of Orestes' crime, which no one in the play comments on except the barbarian Thoas, 1174.

28. *at a separate table*: this passage purports to give the origin of a spring festival at Athens called the Feast of Pitchers. The bracketed lines may be a later addition. However, the reference to this festival

is less significant for the drama than the light thrown on the character of Orestes by his account of his visit to Athens. He feels no indebtedness to the Athenians for receiving a polluted man; and though the events of the play give him every reason for regarding Apollo as a fraud, it seems never to occur to him that he himself bears any responsibility for his crime. His attitude is the same that he shows in the latter half of *Orestes* where, as in this play, his insanity is a factor in the situation.

29. *I appeared before the court* . . . : this famous trial, for which the Court of Areopagus was said to have been founded, is the subject of *The Eumenides*, the third play of Aeschylus' *Oresteian Trilogy*. This speech of Orestes, narrating the personal appearance of the eldest of the Furies and the two Olympian deities on Ares' Hill in Athens, is in curious contrast with the rationalism of the Herdsman, 292-4, and Thoas, 1166.

30. *Or was this his plan* . . . : in the MSS a line is missing here; this sentence is supplied to complete the sense.

31. *Silence!*: The line literally means, 'I have spat out; for I speak this word for the sake of holiness'. If a speaker had heard, or had been tempted to utter, a word which would bring pollution, he could avoid ritual impurity by saying, 'I spit out (the word)'.

32. *who know all things*: literally, 'the more things'; i.e., 'those things which are more than what I have expressed'.

33. *the certainties of heaven*: the last ten lines provide an ironic end to this charming poem. It is true that Iphigenia was wrong in interpreting her dream to mean that Orestes was already dead; but it is also true that the poet shows Apollo as no less untrustworthy. Prayers for help are addressed both to him and to Artemis at various stages in the play; yet neither has the power to save Orestes' ship from being forced back to the shore by Poseidon, so that, as far as the children of Leto are concerned, Orestes is condemned to die today, and the dream was correctly understood. Disaster is only averted by Athena, whose intervention the poet uses ironically in *The Suppliant Women* and *Ion*, and whose arrival in Taurica emphasizes the plight of those who rely on the gods they pray to.

34. *Not till I know for certain* . . . : literally, 'till an interpreter (or "informant") speaks this word'.

35. *at the ready*: literally, 'holding their oars against the tholes'.

36. *for the two men to climb aboard*: the text here is corrupt. There is a phrase about 'passing the stern-cables through their hands', but it is hard to fit this into the sentence.

37. *One of their men*: it is not clear whether the operations described in this and the next line were undertaken by men in the ship, trying to steady her, or by men on shore, trying to haul her in. The memory of the archers, 1377, makes the latter less likely.

38. *how Artemis saved her . . .*: the irony of this line is in tune with everything Euripides says about human sacrifice. It was Artemis who demanded the sacrifice.

39. *Unhappy Iphigenia!*: See note 20.

40. *at my request*: Athena can do what Apollo and Artemis either cannot or will not do — reverse the apparent purpose of Poseidon. See note 33.

41. *this is my command*: after these words at least one line is missing.

42. At the end of the play the MSS add three lines apparently intended to be spoken on behalf of the poet, appealing to *Nikē*, Victory, to grant him the prize awarded for the best play:

Holy, mighty Victory,
Watch my ways and keep my life,
Give me still the poet's crown!

The same lines are found at the end of *The Phoenician Women* and *Orestes*.

FOR THE BEST IN PAPERBACKS, LOOK FOR THE

In every corner of the world, on every subject under the sun, Penguin represents quality and variety – the very best in publishing today.

For complete information about books available from Penguin – including Pelicans, Puffins, Peregrines and Penguin Classics – and how to order them, write to us at the appropriate address below. Please note that for copyright reasons the selection of books varies from country to country.

In the United Kingdom: Please write to *Dept E.P., Penguin Books Ltd, Harmondsworth, Middlesex, UB7 0DA*

In the United States: Please write to *Dept BA, Penguin, 299 Murray Hill Parkway, East Rutherford, New Jersey 07073*

In Canada: Please write to *Penguin Books Canada Ltd, 2801 John Street, Markham, Ontario L3R 1B4*

In Australia: Please write to the *Marketing Department, Penguin Books Australia Ltd, P.O. Box 257, Ringwood, Victoria 3134*

In New Zealand: Please write to the *Marketing Department, Penguin Books (NZ) Ltd, Private Bag, Takapuna, Auckland 9*

In India: Please write to *Penguin Overseas Ltd, 706 Eros Apartments, 56 Nehru Place, New Delhi, 110019*

In Holland: Please write to *Penguin Books Nederland B.V., Postbus 195, NL–1380AD Weesp, Netherlands*

In Germany: Please write to *Penguin Books Ltd, Friedrichstrasse 10–12, D–6000 Frankfurt Main 1, Federal Republic of Germany*

In Spain: Please write to *Longman Penguin España, Calle San Nicolas 15, E–28013 Madrid, Spain*

In France: Please write to *Penguin Books Ltd, 39 Rue de Montmorency, F-75003, Paris, France*

In Japan: Please write to *Longman Penguin Japan Co Ltd, Yamaguchi Building, 2–12–9 Kanda Jimbocho, Chiyoda-Ku, Tokyo 101, Japan*